THE DIVINE INDWELLING

THE DIVINE INDWELLING

Centering Prayer and Its Development

Thomas Keating
Thomas R. Ward, Jr.
Sarah A. Butler
George F. Cairns
Gail Fitzpatrick-Hopler
Paul David Lawson

Lantern Books • New York
A Division of Booklight Inc.

2001
Lantern Books
One Union Square West, Suite 201
New York, NY 10003

Printed in the United States of America

Library of Congress Cataloging-in-Publication Data

The divine indwelling : centering prayer and its development / Thomas Keating ... [et al.]
    p. cm.
Includes bibliographical references.
ISBN 1-930051-79-4 (pbk. : alk. paper)
    1. Contemplation. I. Keating, Thomas.

BV5091 .C7 D585 2001
248.3—dc21

2001045966

Table of Contents

Thomas Keating, O.C.S.O

The Divine Indwelling

ORDINARY LIFE FOR MOST PEOPLE IS CHARACTER-
ized by the sense that God is absent. A little metaphysics
would alert us to the fact that if God were not present at every
moment, we would not be here either. Creation is not a one-
time event in the past. It is the ongoing gift of our being—at
every level—from the humblest quark to the highest stage of
consciousness.

   Saint Teresa of Avila wrote, "All difficulties in prayer can
be traced to one cause: praying as if God were absent." The
conviction that God is absent is something we bring with us
from early childhood and apply to everyday life and to our
lives in general. It gets stronger as we grow up, unless we are
touched by the Gospel and begin the spiritual journey. Our
journey is a process of dismantling the monumental illusion

that God is distant or absent. When our particular petitions are not answered, we become even more convinced that God is absent. This is an irrational position based on the judgment of emotion and not of reason. Unfortunately, unruly emotions do not obey reason and will. They have their own dynamics. Whenever our reason and will decide to do something, our emotions get into a huddle and decide whether or not they will go along with it. If our plan contradicts their perception of what is pleasant or unpleasant, we have a riot on our hands.

The start, middle, and end of the spiritual journey is the conviction that God is always present. As we progress on this journey, God becomes more and more present to us. As we emerge from childhood into a more fully reflective self-consciousness, our concept of how God is present in us is generally vague and primitive. The spiritual journey is a gradual process of enlarging our emotional, mental, and physical relationship with the divine reality that is present in us, but not ordinarily accessible to our emotions or rationalizations.

The dogma of the Trinity speaks to us of one God in three divine persons. The first person is called the Father. The second person is called the Word. The third person is called the Holy Spirit ("spirit" means "breath"). Did you ever know a person who was a "word" or a "breath?" This should alert us to the fact that, when we speak of God, we are not talking about anyone we know in the way that we know people. The concept of persons in God refers to relationships that are *anal-*

ogous to human relationships, not *the same* as them. Therefore, we must not expect God to be "present" in the way human persons are present. Once we begin accepting the mystery of the Trinity by faith, our concepts and feelings about God begin expanding. This education about the nature of God was the chief fruit of the spiritual discipline of the Old Testament. It was a long-term education that gradually weaned the people of Israel away from their narrow concept of God as one among other Near Eastern gods to the Transcendent One. Monotheism is, under God, the great gift of Israel to humanity.

God is present to us all of the time, but God is inaccessible as long as we have preconceived ideas and judgments based solely on the feedback provided by our senses and feelings. The saying of Jesus at the beginning of his ministry might be paraphrased: "The reign of God is close at hand"—not distant or absent. It is in you and in your midst. (cf. Mark 1:15)

The fundamental theological principle of the spiritual journey is the divine indwelling. The Trinity is present within us as the source of our being on every level. Each level of life from the most physical to the most spiritual is sustained by the divine presence. To do liturgy or to pray while thinking that God is absent will prevent us from relating properly to the divine presence.

The reign of God is basically what God does in us. The divine is present as energy sustaining our physical, mental, and spiritual activities without a single moment's interruption.

Jesus calls us to full human development, re-rooting us in our source and enabling us to experience this divine energy as infinitely tender, compassionate, and nurturing. Jesus' experience of the Father as *Abba*, the God of infinite concern and tenderness for every living thing, especially human beings, was rooted deep in the faith and worship of Israel. His understanding was reflected in the commentaries of the fathers of the church. Both need to be made the first lesson in every catechetical instruction and to be constantly repeated in sermons and homilies. The divine indwelling of the Holy Trinity is a truth of faith that is easily forgotten or avoided, yet it is the one on which a radical personal conversion depends.

In our tradition we believe that the Word of God revealed in scripture is addressed to us. That Word also became flesh in order that God's own example would give us a blueprint of how to become fully human and fully divine. This Word of God addresses us through scripture and liturgy to awaken us to God's abiding presence within us. Contemplative prayer is our awakening to this relationship, to what God is doing, has done, and will do for us.

Scripture for the early Christians was not so much read as heard because they did not have printed books. If you only heard the Gospel once a week and were interested in the spiritual journey, you would go to church all ears and listen to the readings with the whole of your being. We have been desensitized to the written Word of God even though we read everything else under the sun. The vitality of sacred scripture does not easily appear to us. We must again convince ourselves that there is a special presence of Christ in scripture that speaks to the hearts of those who are open and prepared. The Holy Spirit nudges us to perceive that what we hear applies to our personal situation and is meant to be a challenge and an encouragement to us. Once we understand that the Gospel is addressed to a presence within us that already exists, listening to the Word of God becomes a process of gradual enlightenment.

The fathers of the church called this process the development of the spiritual senses. The external senses perceive the immediacy of material reality. The reality that the spiritual senses perceive is the immediacy of the divine reality in various forms. As we begin to perceive the divine presence fully, the Word of God is gradually assimilated, interiorized, and understood. As the process advances, the fruits of the Spirit enumerated by Paul in Galatians 5:22–24 and (implicitly) by our Lord in the Beatitudes (Matt. 5:3–11) begin to emerge. These are signs that we are awakening to the divine presence.

The first stage in this process of enlightenment is listening with the undivided attention of one who wants to learn from a great teacher. In the Christian scheme of things, Jesus is the enlightened one who lives in the Christian assembly as the glorified Christ, our teacher. The liturgy juxtaposes texts to awaken us through words and symbols to the divine presence within us and how it operates in our personal lives both in prayer and in action. Prayer, the sacraments, and good works are all directed toward one purpose: to awaken us to who we actually are but do not yet know. The reception of the Eucharist is not a passing visit from Christ, but an awakening to his abiding presence within us, leading us into the further experience of the Father.

The Spirit bears witness to Christ's resurrection by working in us the fruits of the Spirit (Gal. 5:22–23). On the literal level, all we can do is listen to the message with good will and begin the process of dismantling our illusion that God is absent. In daily life the action of the Spirit increases as we try to put the values of the Gospel into effect. The monastics of the Middle Ages called this the moral level of scripture. When we are moved by the beauty and example of the life of Jesus, we take courage that it might be possible to overcome our own emotional programs for happiness, which prevent us from accessing the full light of God's presence and action within us.

When the Word of God addresses us at a deeper level, we move toward an allegorical understanding of scripture. We become aware that the same graces that we are hearing about in the Gospel are taking place in our personal lives. If Jesus could put up with the faults of the apostles, he will surely put up with ours.

At the allegorical level, one begins to understand the deeper meaning of scripture to which Jesus invited his disciples when he said, "If you have ears to hear, please hear," implying that they were not listening at the level that he was addressing. The Word of God is not simply addressed to our ears, to our minds, and to our hearts; it is addressed above all to who we are at the deepest level. We are rooted in God. By accessing that divine energy, we are united to God and able to do what Jesus did: to be a manifestation of God's tenderness and compassion among the people we serve and love.

Seeing the allegorical level awakens us to the fact that Jesus invites us into the commitment of friendship. This commitment opens up the various levels of union that the fathers of the church called "the unitive way." The unitive way is the awareness of the abiding presence of God, a presence that is not undermined by what we feel or think, by what others do, or even by tremendous tragedy. We find our Source. We become the Word of God and express the divine presence, just as Jesus expressed it as he lived his daily life.

Each time we move through faith to a new level of hearing the Word of God, all of our relationships change—toward ourselves, God, other people, and the cosmos. Then we have to spend a considerable length of time integrating all of our relationships into this new perspective.

As we read scripture with an attitude of listening and we respond to it with openness, reflection, and love, we internalize and assimilate the message. In addition, the message moves us to respond to the good things that we have read. Thus, prayer becomes the spontaneous response to the presence of the Word of God. This Word is not only present as a sound but as a person. When we speak of the Word of God, we mean both the written Word of God and the Word of God enfleshed in Jesus. Both Words (which are the *one* Word) are knocking at the door of our inmost being where, because of our weak faith, Christ seems, so to speak, to be asleep. Since we have never or only rarely experienced Christ's presence, we assume that he is absent. As faith grows, that illusion is gradually diminished and healed.

The spiritual journey is often presented as the purification of illusion, as liberation from seeking the wrong things or too much of good things, as freedom from compulsions that arise from the misguided search for happiness—a search that is still present in our unconscious and that manifests itself in upsetting emotions. Afflictive emotions arise when something we do not want happens or when something we want does not happen. Our decision to follow Christ on the conscious level is not enough to heal the wounds of original sin. We bring with us unconscious programs for happiness from early childhood; we are not fully aware of them until we pursue vigorously the spiritual journey, and they continually upset us when they do not achieve their desired objects.

Thus, if power or control is our predominant program for happiness, we can make all the resolutions we want not to be upset by circumstances that are beyond our control, and yet *still* feelings of anger, grief, or discouragement will arise when something we plan is frustrated. We are always struggling with what we want to do or decide to do, and with the feelings that oppose our good resolutions. This is the area that we have to address in daily life. The sense of radiant energy that Christ communicates when his Word has finally resounded at the deepest level within us begins to work its way into all our thinking and activity in order to enhance our capacity to respond with the kind of love that motivated him.

The spiritual journey teaches us three things. First, to believe in the divine indwelling within us, fully present and energizing every level of our being. Second, to recognize that this energy is benign, healing, and transforming. And third, to enjoy its gradual unfolding, step by step, both in prayer and action.

Our prayer, as contemplative persons, is the constant exercise of faith, hope, and charity (divine love), and it takes place in the silence of our hearts as we listen to the Word of God not just with our ears or minds but with our inmost being. God speaks best by silence. This does not mean that we do not have unwanted thoughts during prayer, but that we return again and again to the basic consent of self-surrender and trust in God. We affirm that presence, and every now and again enter into union with it as we identify the divine presence in Christ's humanity with the divine presence within us.

When we say, "Come, Lord Jesus," we should remember that Christ is already here. His coming means that he becomes more and more present to our consciousness. He does not move. We move. This process is one of consent to God's presence, surrender to it, and being transformed by it. As we learn to listen to the Word of God within us, we develop greater sensitivity to the seven gifts of the Spirit, allowing the divine energy to manifest itself appropriately during prayer and in the events of daily life. Jesus comes to us in the Eucharist to be with us all the time and to suggest how we can live our lives in a divine way, according to God's will.

Thomas R. Ward, Jr.

Spirituality and Community: Centering Prayer and the Ecclesial Dimension

"I DON'T KNOW MUCH ABOUT ANY OF YOU, BUT I feel closer to you than I do to anyone else in my life." These words were spoken by a woman with three young children who also worked outside the home. The collective "you" that she addressed was a Centering Prayer support group in a third-floor classroom of a large, vibrant, downtown Episcopal parish in which I served as rector. This woman had been a faithful member of that weekly support group for five years. She had sat in the silence of Centering Prayer with many of those others throughout that time. Her words had a ring of authenticity about them, and they evoked the assent of others in the group: many bore witness that they too sensed an intimacy among those gathered that was not dependent on the usual exchange of social conversation. There was an attitude of wonder that such bondedness could occur through the accumulated experience of the group. I facilitated this group.

Having discovered Centering Prayer while on sabbatical in the late 1980s, I had begun teaching it in the parish and convening a weekly group. I wanted to offer to others what I had received, but I also needed support for the practice myself. I took seriously Thomas Keating's counsel: one needs such a group for encouragement, accountability, and continuing education.[1] Indeed, after offering this practice to hundreds of people over the past twelve years, I have found few who continue for very long without such a group. There seems to be something about contemplative prayer that necessitates gathering with others who are called to respond to God in the same way.

More than any other group in our parish, this Centering Prayer support group met the yearning for "spirituality" and "community" that I had often heard parishioners and others desiring but not finding—in spite of all sorts of programs being offered and after persons trying one group after another. The Centering Prayer group also fed my hunger for a community based on the contemplative dimension of the Gospel. Those participating could pray silently, entering into intimacy with God and one another, without others crossing their personal boundaries and intruding into their inner core.

I might add at this point that the same bondedness emerges in the retreats that Thomas Keating and his staff designed. Generally, about twenty persons spend ten days in silence together, practicing Centering Prayer from four-and-a-half to six hours a day. One fruit of this work is the experience of community that emerges among the participants—in spite of the fact that there is little or no talking. While it is clear that there are many differences among the participants, differences that would have to be resolved in conversation if the group were to attempt to continue its life together, it is also clear that those participating in these retreats know a unity in silence that allows their individual differences to be transcended.[2]

"I don't know much about any of you, but I feel closer to you than I do to anyone else in my life." Over the years I have reflected on this woman's words and their aptness for what most of us in that group experienced. As I do this, Thomas Merton's description of his epiphany on the streets of Louisville, Kentucky, also comes to mind.

In Louisville, at the corner of Fourth and Walnut, in the center of the shopping district, I was suddenly overwhelmed with the realization that I loved all those people, that they were mine and I theirs, that we could not be alien to one another even though we were total strangers....

It is a glorious destiny to be a member of the human race....

Now I realize what we all are. And if only everybody could realize this! But it cannot be explained. There is no way of telling people that they are all walking around shining like the sun.[3]

Merton goes on to reflect on a paradox: he has entered the monastery and gone apart from the world and the people in it, but he has become "one with them." Through his solitude, he has come to see all other human beings as his "own self." Then he generalizes about all others from the perspective of his contemplative experience:

At the center of our being is a point of nothingness which is untouched by sin and by illusion, a point of pure truth, a point or spark which belongs entirely to God....This little point of nothingness and of *absolute poverty* is the pure glory of God in us....It is like a pure diamond, blazing with the invisible light of heaven. It is in everybody....I have no program for this seeing. It is only given. But the gate of heaven is everywhere.[4]

It is as if by entering his own center—through the rhythms of monastic life and the contemplative prayer it fosters—that Merton has touched the ground where God and humankind meet. Spirituality and community come together.

Roberta Bondi articulates this groundedness through sixth-century monastic Dorotheus of Gaza.

> Once, the brothers in the monastery of Dorotheus of Gaza forgot what they were about in the monastic life....Dorotheus reminded them: "Suppose we were to take a compass and insert the point and draw the outline of a circle. The center point is the same distance from any point on the circumference....Let us suppose that this circle is the world and that God is the center; the straight lines drawn from the circum-ference to the center are the lives of [human beings]...."

> Let us assume for the sake of the analogy that to move toward God, then, human beings move from the circumference along the various radii of the circle to the center. "But at the same time, the closer they are to God, the closer they become to one another; and the closer they are to one another, the closer they become to God."[5]

The image of circle, center, and radii obviously fits Merton's language and the language of Centering Prayer. Each person moves Godward through grace. Part of that movement is inward to one's personal center, but another part is toward others through God. The fathers and mothers of the church never tired of using Psalm 42:7 as a means of describing intimacy with God and neighbor: "Deep calls to deep at the thunder of your cataracts." Or, to use the language of Thomas Keating, each true self speaks to another.[6] So it is that one has the sense of knowing and being known.

The Centering Prayer movement emerged as a response to lay seekers coming to the monks of St. Joseph's Monastery in Spencer, Massachusetts, asking the brothers to teach them to pray. It has attracted persons from various backgrounds who yearn for spirituality and community. The movement attempts to translate the essence of monastic spirituality into a form that might appeal to the particular cultural circumstances of our day.[7] It obviously feeds the hunger that many have for a spirituality that reaches into the depths of the individual but that also draws that person more deeply into community with others in the group—and potentially with *all* others.

As an Episcopal priest who came to this prayer in mid-life, I have been especially interested in its ecclesial dimension. Specifically, I would like to see a Centering Prayer support group in every local congregation. Viewed from another perspective, I would not like to see this movement, which has such life-enhancing potential for the life of the Body, go its own way, apart from the institutional church, in all of its forms. It has much to offer every congregation and poses little threat to any of them—unless the power of the Gospel is itself a threat. The reason for my concern lies in the history of the contemplative dimension of the Gospel[8] and my own experience of offering this prayer. In spite of the hunger of many lay persons for spirituality and community, the leadership of many congregations and judicatories is strangely unresponsive. It is not that these issues are not of concern; it is that issues of institutional maintenance are higher on the list of priorities.

Elsewhere I have described Centering Prayer as both preparation for and an extension of participation in the Holy Eucharist.[9] I have done so for two reasons. First, I believe Centering Prayer is both of these things. Second, I wish to counter the familiar contention that those practicing Centering Prayer withdraw from the church and the needs of the world for whose salvation our Lord died. In Centering Prayer we enter into intimacy with one another through intimacy with God. The classic text here is the account of our Lord's prayer given in John 17:21–23. In prayers for his followers, he says, that they may all be one. As you, Father, are in me and I am in you, may they also be in us, so that the world may believe that you have sent me. The glory that you have given me I have given them, so that they may be one as we are one, I in them and you in me, that they may become completely one so that the world may know that you have sent me and have loved them even as you have loved me.

The setting of this passage is the last meal that Jesus ate with his disciples before his crucifixion. The eucharistic context is therefore evident. Beyond this, the passage has an interesting slant on evangelism: the world will come to faith in Christ by witnessing the unity of the church. Sadly, we have all experienced the fragmentation of the church much more than we have seen its unity—which may well be a significant factor leading to the hunger for spirituality and community that is so prevalent in the institutional life of the churches as well as in the life of the world outside the churches.

Our Lord's words also lead to reflection on relations among the persons of the Trinity, an understanding of which the church evolved in succeeding centuries. While an explication of that history is neither possible nor desirable here, it is important to note that the unity of the Church as the Body of Christ, which we affirm in the Nicene Creed, is grounded in the inner life of the Trinity. The unity among the three persons of the Trinity is the basis for the unity of the Church, which, in turn, is the basis for unity when two or three are gathered together in Jesus' name.

One of the most beautiful books I know catches the relation among spiritual growth, trinitarian love, and service in the world.

> Spiritual progress has no other test in the end, nor any better expression, than our ability to love. It has to be unselfish love founded on respect, a service, a disinterested affection that does not asked to be paid in return, a "sympathy," indeed an "empathy" that takes us out of ourselves enabling us to "feel with" the other person and indeed to "feel" in him or her. It gives us the ability to discover in the other person an inward nature as mysterious and deep as our own, but different and willed so by God....The criterion of the depth of one's spiritual growth is therefore love for one's enemies, in accordance with the paradoxical commandment of the Gospel that takes its meaning solely from the cross—Christ's cross and ours—and from the resurrection—again Christ's and our own.... The true miracle, the most difficult achievement, is therefore the example and practice of love....To enter into God is to let oneself be caught up in the immense movement of the love of the Trinity which reveals the

other person to us as "neighbor" or (and this is better)
which enables each one of us to become the "neighbor" of others. And to become a "neighbor" is to side
with Christ, since he identifies himself with every
human being who is suffering and rejected, or impris-
oned, or ignored."[10]

"I don't know much about any of you, but I feel closer to
you than I do to anyone else in my life." The woman who said
those words to our Centering Prayer support group was
evidently onto something very old and very new, and her
words ring with greater depth the longer I ponder them.

Thomas Keating writes that Centering Prayer is based on
three theological principles:

> Its *source* is Trinitarian, its *focus* is Christological, and
> its effects are *ecclesial*, that is, it bonds us with every-
> one else in the Mystical Body of Christ and indeed
> with the whole human family.[11]

These three principles are interrelated: to focus on one of
them leads to the other two. Our experience in the Centering Prayer support group was the ecclesial dimension of the
prayer. We were bonded with one another in a way that
differed from our usual ways of being with others, both inside
the institutional church and outside, and it defied the usual

categories we used to describe our experience of community. That led some of us to see what we experienced there in terms of the parish Eucharist and in terms of Jesus' relation to the One whom he called Father. And this in turn led some to a reflection of the Church's experience of God as Trinity: unity in diversity, the model of the Church as the mystical Body of Christ and the paradigm of human community that is true to itself and its source. I might add that some of those participating in the support group were among the most active in the parish's ministries to the sick and suffering and to those in chronic need in the world. So the bonding we knew in the time of prayer led many to become active "neighbors" to anonymous others in our midst and on our doorstep.

A final aspect of the bonding power of Centering Prayer is its relation to the communion of saints. Just as praying with others in a support group or retreat setting leads to a deep sense of intimacy with the others in the group, practicing Centering Prayer also leads to a feeling of connectedness with those we love who have died. Thomas Keating puts it this way:

> The process of bonding throws light on what we mean by the doctrine of the Communion of Saints...by becoming present to the present, we become present to everyone in the past and in the future and become their friend....The Communion of Saints includes not

only those who are canonized, but also your friends, parents, and ancestors. They are all together now in the love of God. Through contemplative prayer, we are moving into a realm of reality that influences the past and the future perhaps more than anything else we could do.[12]

Before I had ever heard of Centering Prayer, I was taken with a quotation by Thomas Merton from an informal talk he gave to some Eastern monks on the monastic life in Calcutta two months before his death. It ends with these words:

At the deepest level of communication is not communication, but communion. It is wordless. It is beyond words, and it is beyond speech, and it is beyond concept. Not that we discover a new unity. My dear brothers, we are already one. But we imagine that we are not. And what we have to recover is our original unity. What we have to be is what we are.[13]

In that final journey to the East in general and in this talk in particular, Merton attempts to find the common ground with others across barriers of culture, language, and religion without sacrificing his own particularity or that of the other—in this case, the Eastern monks. The communion he mentions comes through his contemplative practice.

Through this practice he reaches the original unity that Eastern monks know through their silent practices. This is the bonding experience with the whole human family to which Thomas Merton alludes in the quotation above. It is available to all of us. "What we have to be is what we are." In our day we yearn for a spirituality that is both true to a particular tradition and that can enter into relation with all others through that tradition. That was what attracted me to this passage when I first read it, and that is among the aspects of Centering Prayer that continues to appeal to my heart.

Nothing is simpler than being what we are, and nothing is more difficult. We need a practice to take us from here to there. Centering prayer is one such practice. While the heart of this practice comes through our going into our room and shutting the door and praying to our Father who is in secret (Matt. 6:6), one effect is the recovery of our original unity, which puts us in a place to join in communion with the original unity of all others, whatever their differences. It gives us a way of entering the dance with our Triune God and of joining others in that bonding experience of communion. The barriers that separate us in the church and in the world—which we Christians say have already been overcome through Christ Jesus our Lord—are more likely to be transcended through our beginning with shared contemplation than they are through our beginning with doctrinal or political debate, as important as these are. The silence opens us to the Other who is in our midst and who wills that all be one.

"I don't know much about any of you, but I feel closer to you than I do to anyone else in my life." Such a beginning might take us to our original unity, to communion.

1. Thomas Keating, *Open Mind, Open Heart: The Contemplative Dimension of the Gospel* (New York: Continuum, 1993), 135–36.
2. For a listing of retreat offerings throughout the country and for further information about Centering Prayer, contact the international office of Contemplative Outreach Limited at (973) 838–3384, or visit their website at www.contemplativeoutreach.org.
3. Thomas Merton, *Conjectures of a Guilty Bystander* (Garden City, NY: Image Books, 1968), 156–57.
4. Ibid., 158.
5. Roberta C. Bondi, *To Pray and to Love: Conversations on Prayer with the Early Church* (Minneapolis, MN: Fortress, 1991), 14–15.
6. Keating, *Open Mind, Open Heart*, 127.
7. Thomas Keating, *Intimacy with God* (New York: Continuum, 1995), 11–21.
8. See, for example, Willigis Jäger, *Search for the Meaning of Life: Essays and Reflections on the Mystical Experience* (Ligouri, MO: Triumph Books, 1995), 128–130.
9. Thomas R. Ward, Jr. "Centering Prayer: An Overview," *STR* 40:1 (Christmas 1996), 27.
10. Olivier Clement, *The Roots of Christian Mysticism: Text and Commentary* (London: New City, 1995), 270–71.
11. Keating, *Intimacy with God*, 148.
12. Ibid., 156–57.
13. Naomi Barton, Patrick Hart, *et al.*, eds. *The Asian Journal of Thomas Merton* (New York: New Directions, 1975), 308.

Sarah A. Butler

Lectio Divina *as a Tool for Discernment*

OVER THE PAST FEW YEARS LAY PEOPLE OF ALL denominations have begun to embrace the time-honored prayer practice of *lectio divina*, or "sacred reading." More than simply reading the Holy Scriptures, it is a way of praying and receiving the Word of God. It invites us to explore the biblical text for understanding a deeper relationship with Christ. Taking a portion of the biblical text, the process is as follows:

Read (*lectio*): Read the story that is told in God's Word. Be present to the Word. Listen to it for information. Digest it. Absorb it.

Reflect (*meditatio*): Become actively involved with the story. Pay attention to what attracts your attention. Notice your own feelings. Reflect on your own inner experience of the scripture. Allow the Gospel (or other text) to be a mirror of your own life.

Respond (*oratio*): Be free to express what is pouring out of the reflection—praise, tears, repentance, thanksgiving, and so on. How is God becoming formed in you? Celebrate this with acceptance.

Rest (*contemplatio*): Let go of all reflections and responses in order to allow God to speak to you in the mystery of silence and quiet presence. Surrender to the mystery.[1]

A few years ago I adapted the four-fold method of *lectio divina*—read, reflect, respond, and rest—to the pastoral care relationship. I found that it helped me establish trusting and compassionate relationships with people in my care if I practiced the same listening rhythm with them as I did when engaging *lectio divina*.[2] The structure itself calls the caregiver to an approach to listening that is patient, humble, and respectful, recognizing that God is the initiator of healing and faith. With our caring ministers at St. John's Cathedral, it has proven a useful way to maintain the integrity of a nondirective, compassionate, caring relationship, and it helps to break down the division between prayer and action in ministry. Just as praying with scripture reveals more fully God's loving intent and forms our identity, so listening to a person in pain in this prayerful mode moves both care-receiver and caregiver to experience God's embrace in the midst of suffering.[3]

Applying "Lectio Divina" to Spiritual Discernment

Recently, I have come to appreciate and apply the rhythms and structure of *lectio divina* to the process of spiritual discernment. Much of life is lived "once-over-lightly," or, as Stephen Covey says, we are involved in the "thick of thin things."[3] We answer the urgent rather than attend to the essential, and too often we make our decisions in reaction to the overwhelming demands of the world. What we seek is a place for renewal and a space to get in touch with our deepest identity in God. Out of that depth flow actions and attitudes that are free from our cultural and personal assumptions. The practice offered here draws us into a rhythm and dynamic that allows for a slow, thoughtful, prayerful drink at the well of life. It honors our uniqueness and recognizes God's facility for surprise. It is Spirit-filled and Spirit-led rather than culturally driven. It presupposes a disposition for faith and a preference for encounter with God rather than a need for direct answers and guidance.

There is no way of getting around the necessity for structures and disciplines in the spiritual life. Rather than imposing a burden, they open and support deeper knowledge of God's love. Just as physical structures sometimes house things that are more valuable than the building itself, so spiritual practices house an environment in which the most precious gift of all, a relationship with Christ, can be nurtured. Colossians 2:17–19 reminds us of the subordination of structures to substance. The author talks about various religious practices, festivals, the observance of the Sabbath, and so on. He places them in their proper perspective: "These are only a shadow of what is to come, but the substance belongs to Christ" (2:17). Disciplines, however valuable, will always be less valuable than our encounter with God. As in any artistic endeavor, it will require hard work and commitment. We are beginning to understand how God speaks to us in the everyday events of life, and it is worthwhile listening carefully to the conversation. The following reflects my own application of this particular discipline:

Read: Gather in all the information. Get the facts, the figures and the who, what, where, and how of the situation. This is great for left-brain types who can even make a list of all the facts in a journal. Beware, though, of remaining in the left-brain function. The Holy Spirit has a tendency to perplex, to disarm, and to confound linear thinking. Information is only the beginning of the full formation needed to take place. Spend some time mulling over the information with no judgments or conclusions.

Reflect: Now begin to notice what your mind has "highlighted" in your story. What gets your attention? What resistance do you notice? Use your imagination to reflect upon the various directions and how they might unfold for you and for others. Notice your sensory reactions. What does it sound, taste, look, smell, and feel like? Spend time "woolgathering."

Respond: Now flow into your inner experience. How do you feel about the situation? What is your intuition telling you? What signs are coming forth in the body of Christ? Notice the coincidences that are becoming providential. What do you think God is communicating to you? What sound judgments are beginning to emerge? Wait, God is not finished with you yet! Offer up all of the above to God with open hands and open heart. You may well be moved to prayers of thanksgiving and praise as you experience God's presence in this area of your life. Even the gift of God's guidance gives way to the appreciation of just being with God. Spend time in open, silent, receptive prayer.

Rest: Let go to the mystery of God's love and action working in you. We do this by letting go of the need to know or control outcomes. We keep offering up our reflections and responses until we sense the peace that God will indeed do "greater things than we can ask or imagine."

This may seem at first glance to be a method too centered on the self to be useful, but where else are we to begin? Even when we begin with an agenda or a heart focused on a particular result, the process itself acts as a corrective if we exercise faith in God's wisdom. Genuine prayer has a way of allowing

God to transform our deepest desires so they may be made compatible with God's vision for us in the kingdom. As Douglas Steere wrote, "It [prayer] has changed my mind when I did not mean to change it. It has firmed me up when I might have yielded. It has rested me. It has upset my sluggish rest."[4] We seldom end where we begin. The gospels support this in the drama of encounters with Jesus. I have noticed that in many of the dialogues, people asked Jesus left-brain questions, and he gave them right-brain answers. He gave the question back to them and/or he engaged in a dialogue that elicited a faith response. In the story of the woman at the well (John 4:7–29), Jesus perplexes her with statements that at first glance do not seem to make a great deal of sense. He speaks of living water and of never thirsting again. He refers to eternal life while she wonders where he has his waterpot. As the dialogue proceeds, however, Jesus shifts to her personal life and reveals her pain, her disappointments, and her longings. At the conclusion of this long conversation filled with mystery, metaphor, and private revelations, she runs to tell others she has found the Christ.

The healing of the man at Bethesda is an example of Jesus asking a question in order to confront the man's thirty-eight-year failure to be the first in the pool (John 5:3–9). Did his illness draw sympathy and become his identity? Had he become a martyr as people pitied his misfortune year after year? Jesus found it necessary to ask, "Do you want to be made well?" How many of us have been asked the same, "Do you really want what you're praying for?"

We too want to ask a straightforward question and receive a simple and timely reply from God. Although prayers and questions of guidance are not like fast-food orders for Jesus, we must be able to verbalize our straightforward needs as the first "reading" of our own yearnings, needs, and search for purpose. Just as one reading of scripture fails to reveal all the nuances of meaning, the initial interpretation of a life event or question is inadequate either to explore all its facets or, more importantly, to meet and invite God as our divine companion. God wants our prayers to be a conversation, facilitating self-awareness, deeper faith responses, and increased compassion for others. It is not out of the ordinary to discover that one's focus shifts from the need to know answers to the appreciation of a growing companionship with God.

A few years ago I was considering a position that would require a major move. I spent much time in prayer and reflection, examining my feelings. I found myself asking for the two-hundredth time the straightforward question, "Lord should I make this move?" The reply I "heard" from the Holy Spirit was: "I don't care where you go. I'll be with you here, and I'll be with you there." I did not interpret this to mean a lack of interest from God or that there was no preferred path, but I received this graced affirmation from God as a reminder that the substance of my spiritual path is to love and be loved by God. This reality gives life to all of the directions and decisions and actions I choose. In fact, the assurance of that loving union enables me to trust my intuitions as being divinely grounded and inspired. God's loving initiative can be conveyed through infinite ways, venues, and vocations.

Not only does this structure encourage a growing trust in God, it also provides us with a growing trust in ourselves. We probably have no problem believing that nature is a medium of God's activity. Although we are products of nature, subject to its laws, we are also mediators of the grace of the Holy Spirit. Too often we forget that grace works through our own natural faculties. The practice I have offered here, by virtue of its repetition and invitation to spend "quality time" with God, cultivates an ability to recognize more readily the Spirit's urgings. It extends the meaning of the Incarnation to include us: "Very truly, I tell you, the one who believes in me will also do the works that I do and, in fact, will do greater works than these, because I am going to the Father" (John 14:12).

The gift of the incarnation was the restoration of God's self-communication through the physical sphere. Burning bushes, partings of great seas, and other such supernatural phenomena are nothing compared with our knowledge of the reality of the resurrected presence of Christ within us. Submitting ourselves to spiritual disciplines sharpens our faculties and enables us to trust our interpretations, recognizing the profound meaning at the heart of our experience. In Charles Dickens's *A Christmas Carol*, when Scrooge is visited by Marley's ghost, he is unable at first to interpret the vision: he thinks it is just a bit of undigested beef. In the same way we are inclined to misinterpret our perceptions unless we hone our spiritual faculties by methods that nurture relationship with God. We do not want to find ourselves in the position of dismissing a deep spiritual yearning as indigestion; nor do we want to deny that our natural processes of body and mind may be agents of spiritual realities. God does not confine divine grace and activity to just one mode, and it is incumbent upon us to be alert to the ever-fresh ways of the Spirit's movement.

The discipline that I have tried to describe offers just one more faithful and mature way to reflect upon life's experience. All people have positive and negative experiences, but not everyone grows as a result. Self-understanding and wisdom are not automatic during a time of transition but are facilitated by intentional reflection upon the experience and by the attempt to integrate it into life in a faithful and mature way.

As union with God deepens through a variety of spiritual disciplines, the challenge to become participants in the continuation of Christ's mission is realized. God is like a good parent who wants to empower sons and daughters to become adults. Spiritual toddlers, by contrast, want God to be Superman, swooping in to eliminate anything that puts them in harm's way. I heard a true story a few years ago that never fails to delight me. A woman had picked up her daughter at school and got her car stuck in the muddy parking lot. The harder she tried to get out, the deeper her wheels sank. She turned to her little girl and pleaded "Honey, will you say a prayer and ask God to help us get out of the mud?" She bowed her head and whispered her silent request. Just as she raised her head, her mother maneuvered the car easily out of the mud. "Whatever did you say to God?" the astonished mother asked. "I asked God *please* to make you a better driver" was the wise reply. What, after all, best serves us in the long run, supernatural intervention or becoming "better drivers" spiritually?

We are made in God's image for more than personal consolations: we are on a sacred journey. Our faith formation is certainly to help us grow in the knowledge and love of God and also to demonstrate to the world by our lives the power of Christ working within us. We are beneficiaries of a rich spiritual tradition developed over two thousand years to enable us to live in the fullness of God's love. The application of *lectio divina* to the process of discernment is just one among a variety of disciplines available to those who seek to "be transformed by the renewing of your minds, so that you may discern what is the will of God—what is good and acceptable and perfect" (Rom. 12:2)

1. See Sarah A. Butler, "Pastoral Care and Centering Prayer," *STR* 40:1 (Christmas 1996), 60–61.
2. Ibid., 57–61.
3. Steven Covey in the audiotape, "The Seven Habits of Highly Effective People" (Provo, UT: Covey Leadership Center, 1996).
4. Douglas Van Steere, *Traveling In: Poems about Popper*, 1988–1995, E. Glenn Hinson, ed. (Wallingford, PA: Pendle Hill, 1995), 18–19.

George F. Cairns

A Dialogue Between Centering Prayer and Transpersonal Psychology

READERS OF THIS BOOK MAY BE FAMILIAR WITH the method and underlying theological framework for Centering Prayer, a practice recovered from the monastic tradition by Father Thomas Keating and others.[1] This practice has been contextualized for contemporary people who live busy lives in the world. I have written elsewhere about introducing Centering Prayer in an ecumenical seminary curriculum.[2]

In this paper I would like to address a critical concern that I have both as a practical theologian and as a scientist. As a psychologist for nearly thirty years and, more recently, as a practical theologian for the past fifteen years or so, I am troubled that there has been so little discourse between scientific psychology and Christian contemplative practice.

Two good counterexamples to this state of affairs are, however, provided in the work of Thomas Keating in spiritual theology and Ken Wilber in transpersonal psychology.[3] While Wilber has drawn most of his examples from Eastern spirituality, he provides some bridges to Western Christianity as well. Keating has integrated Wilber's work into his evolutionary model of human development, which he also offers as a model for the Christian spiritual journey. I hope to continue this conversation by extending it to include the philosopher Gregory Bateson.

Transpersonal Psychology

Transpersonal psychology offers both theory and method for this conversation, and for the past twenty-five years it has offered a number of insights into the nature of spiritual practice.[4] This "fourth force"[5] in American psychology was described in 1969 by one of its founders, Anthony J. Sutich, as being

> concerned specifically with the *empirical*, scientific study of, and responsible implementation of the findings relevant to, becoming, individual and species-wide meta-needs, ultimate values, unitive consciousness, peak experiences, B-values, ecstasy, mystical

experience, awe, being, self-actualization, essence, bliss, wonder, ultimate meaning, transcendence of the self, spirit, oneness, cosmic awareness, individual and species-wide synergy, maximal interpersonal encounter, sacralization of everyday life, transcendental phenomena, cosmic self-humor and playfulness; maximum sensory awareness, responsiveness and expression; and related concepts, experiences and activities.[6]

In spite of its many contributions, this field of study continues to struggle with self-definition. In a recent review Denise Lajoie and S. I. Shapiro offer the following "precise and contemporary" definition of transpersonal psychology: "Transpersonal psychology is concerned with the study of humanity's highest potential, and with the recognition, understanding, and realization of unitive, spiritual, and transcendent states of consciousness."[7]

While I am largely in agreement with this definition, I believe that the work of Gregory Bateson offers us ideas to clarify further the nature of these states, to describe their relationships elegantly and coherently from an epistemological perspective, and to provide heuristic clues for an empirical study of these phenomena. In particular, I believe that his notions of mental process or mind offer us insights regarding the nature of the *trans* in transpersonal, and his notions of learning point to ways in which we can understand common elements of spiritual practice.

Gregory Bateson's Notions of Mind

Central to Bateson's thought is that he regards mind as a relational process rather than a thing (a disengaged process called "mind") contained within another thing (the brain/body). While highly formal and abstract, his criteria for mind have profound implications for religious experience. Bateson's notion of mind involves a process of communication in the broadest sense, triggered by difference, utilizing collateral energy, and requiring circular or more complex chains of communication, along with transformations of information.[8]

I will highlight only one aspect of his relational conception of mind here—that mind is not limited to the process contained within a single individual human organism:

> There is no requirement of a clear boundary, like a surrounding envelope of skin or membrane, and you can recognize that this definition [of mind] includes only some of the characteristics of what we call "life." As a result, it applies to a much wider range of those complex phenomena called "systems," including systems consisting of multiple organisms or systems in which some of the parts are living and some are not, or even to systems in which there are no living parts.[9]

I have detailed elsewhere some eco-spiritual implications of this radically different view of what constitutes mind.[10] Let me emphasize here that this view requires that we regard mind as an interpenetrating process that includes different people and other actors at different times. Thus, it requires that we eliminate the view that our mind is only the process that resides within the boundary of our physical body and is somehow radically separate from other minds.

This is an understanding amazingly similar to the deeply relational theology that Keating describes as the underlying process of Centering Prayer. This view is succinctly presented by Keating in his definition of contemplative prayer: "Contemplative Prayer is the opening of mind and heart— our whole being—to God, the ultimate mystery, beyond thoughts, words, and emotions."[11] For him, prayer is most deeply about relationship, opening ourselves to the mystery of God and being permeable to God's guiding Spirit in our lives.

Of course, Bateson and Keating are not alone in this appreciation of the relational embeddedness of human existence in all of creation. Many contemplatives in the world's religious traditions have reported similar experiences.[12] In a recent book aptly titled *Belonging to the Universe*, Fritjof Capra, David Steindl-Rast, and Thomas Matus present an elegant discussion of the emerging contemplative and scientific understanding of this profound engagement.[13]

One implication of Bateson's notion of mind is that, to the extent that the patterns of relationship we call minds do connect, similar methods for change may bring about the transformation of individual human beings as well as larger systems in which they are embedded. On the other hand, the same unifying concepts offer clues to the stability of systems and the difficulty they experience meeting challenges.

I believe that both Keating[14] and Bateson suggest hopeful possibilities for what can happen when we come together in religious communities. They indicate that community greatly enhances the possibility of our becoming more fully human. Perhaps the process of becoming more fully the people that God intends us to be may be understood, at least partially, in an organic, orderly, and analytic way. In short, this emerging view of mind suggests that, when we come together in communities of reflection, accountability, and action, we have the *possibility* of engaging one another in as profound and integrative a way as our individual bodies themselves are integrated.[15]

Why is it that we have such difficulty experiencing this state of belonging to each other and to all of creation? How is it that we seem so often to be locked into lives that isolate us from others? Bateson provides us with clues here as he examines how minds learn.

Bateson's Notion of Learning
and the Theory of Logical Types

Bateson applied Bertrand Russell's "Theory of Logical Types" to the concept of learning.[16] His intent, as is mine, is "that the barriers of misunderstanding which divide the various species of behavioral scientists [including contemplatives and transpersonal psychologists] can be illuminated" by such notions.[17] Russell's theory states:

> No class can, in formal logical or mathematical discourse, be a member of itself; that a class of classes cannot be one of the classes which are its members; that a name is not the thing named....
>
> Somewhat less obvious is the further assertion of the theory: that a class cannot be one of those items which are correctly classified as its nonmembers....
>
> Lastly, the theory asserts that if these simple rules of formal discourse are contravened, paradox will be generated and the discourse vitiated.[18]

The theory proposes a hierarchy of more and more abstract classes with less abstract classes nested within higher-order classes. For example, the class "table" is of one level of logical type, and the class "non-table" is of the same level. They are both nested within the logical class "furniture," which is a class of the classes table and non-table. If one formally attempts to treat the logical class "furniture" the same as its class members "table" or "non-table," logical problems arise. Please understand that there is no priority or greater positive value associated with classes that are more abstract or which contain nested classes within them.

For simplicity of presentation I will use examples of individual organisms' learning below. The reader should remember that Bateson's notion of mental process includes systems of multiple organisms and nonliving elements. Also let me continue to stress that learning in Bateson's use of the term is not limited to cognitive rational processes. Learning includes all processes by which minds learn. As will be detailed below, much, if not all, learning takes place outside our awareness.

Classes of Learning Types: Bateson applied this notion to describe a set of classes of learning labeled "Learning I" through "Learning III." Each higher class contains within it the lower classes of learning.[19]

Learning I: This is what we mean by the term "learning" in common usage. "These are the cases in which an entity gives at Time 2 a different response from what it gave at Time 1."[20] This concept covers a broad range of learning, from a pigeon learning which button to peck in an experiment to a person learning to play Bach on the harpsichord. Learning I requires that new responses occur after repeated practice. These kinds of learning are called by psychologists and others trial-and-error learning, instrumental learning, or conditioning.

Learning II: This next higher type involves learning about learning: "Various terms have been proposed in the literature for various phenomena of this order. 'Deutero-learning,' 'set learning,' 'learning to learn,' and 'transfer of learning' may be mentioned."[21] This is learning about the context in which learning takes place. For example, when I first learn to play a piece on the harpsichord, it may take me a long time to play it with few errors (Learning I). As I continue to play new pieces, the speed of learning to the same level of performance will increase (Learning II). I have learned a class of behaviors, "harpsichord playing," and can transfer learned skills from one member of that class, "Bach fugue," to another, "Vivaldi concerto."

As described in more detail below, much of this kind of learning takes place outside awareness. Learned patterns may become more and more generalized and ultimately may color a person's global expectations. The person may then anticipate that the world is mostly baroque, structured, or chaotic. Bateson argues that these more general relational patterns develop early and also quickly drop out of awareness.[22] Keyboard artists often point to this intuition when they say that playing "gets into the hands" or that someone who specializes in a particular class of musical material develops deep sensitivities for the period (and sometimes has difficulty shifting to different periods). Bateson suggests that what is learned is "a way of *punctuating events*."[23] What then happens is that we often engage our world "to fit the expected punctuation."[24] This self-validating process is difficult to erode because it drops out of awareness, and the person unconsciously limits seeing the possibilities for other punctuation and/or manipulates the environment and misses other learning opportunities. Preferences develop and emotions, both positive and negative, begin to be associated with the particular punctuation/divisions that emerge in the developing world of the individual.

This process can be so pervasive and entrenched that it leads to primary attributes of an individual's personality. "In describing individual human beings, both the scientist and the layman commonly resort to adjectives descriptive of 'character' " to denote the results of Learning II.[25] I believe that this process is very much like what Thomas Keating calls the development of the "false self system."[26] What takes place in Learning II is that life experiences become truncated by degraded perception and by limitations on action. Human freedom is thus eroded and the fullness of creation is constrained by our developing what Keating calls "programs for happiness" that further undermine our full relationships with all of creation and ultimately with God.[27]

Learning III: Keating describes "divine therapy" as a grace-filled healing that God offers us as our spiritual practice of Centering Prayer continues.[28] I believe that the learning processes that facilitate this healing have resonances in the process that Bateson calls Learning III, and I extend an examination of these processes to include Learning IV.

Learning III is expanding the set of alternatives that are currently available to us, or, as Bateson states, *"Learning III is change in the process of Learning II*, e.g., a corrective change in the system of sets of alternatives from which choice is made."[29] This is a powerful shift in perspective or a breakthrough in understanding—we are literally "gifted" with a new way of being. Previously constricted perceptions are now unbound, and new ways of acting become possible. Bateson observes,

> Learning III is likely to be difficult and rare even in human beings. Expectably, it will also be difficult for scientists, who are only human, to imagine or describe this process. But it is claimed that something of the sort does from time to time occur in psychotherapy, religious conversion, and in other sequences in which there is profound reorganization of character.[30]

Others have argued that similar openings to transformation are much more frequent but are "so very short-lived that they go unnoticed."[31] I am optimistic that such openings are even more frequent and may be sustained for more extended periods. I have written elsewhere how these openings take place in lives of supposedly ordinary people, suggesting how they can be sustained in communities of learners.[32]

All of these views suggest that we need supports for our individual and collective memories. I believe one such community of support and accountability is the Contemplative Outreach organization founded by Keating and others.

Learning IV: I argue that there is a least one higher-order class of learning, Learning IV, that has as its primary characteristic the ability to move freely among all of the lower levels of learning and, in particular, that would make readily available the multiple shifts in perspective of the sorts described in Learning III. The multiperspectival worldviews called the "intuitive" by Wilber and Keating undercut our cultural-mythic membership mentality and may allow nuanced perceptions and activities that are almost never seen outside specific cultural boundaries. I am talking here about a true multiperspectival process in which one can approach full entry into different cultural and perceptual worlds.

If speaking about Learning III is difficult, attempting to describe Learning IV is even more perilous. The very definition of Learning IV, with its the ability to cross boundaries of different learning types, suggests that paradoxes and other logical difficulties by definition arise from attempting to capture these phenomena in logical discourse. This theory implies that much of the "ineffability" of such mystical experience may not lie in the phenomenology of the experience itself. Rather, the difficulty of expressing experiences of Learning IV in logical discourse reflects an epistemological limitation of what it is to be human. Experiences that are simultaneously true at different levels of learning appear to be contradictory or paradoxical when we reflect on them. I also wonder if Learning IV and higher classes of learning resonate with the notion of the "spiritual senses," where the immediacy of the experience may only be described in words by analogy.[33]

Some Final Thoughts

What is the usual primary vantage point for us as human beings? It is the context for learning that we call "the self," which usually evolves into "the false self system." Associations are made between the literally infinite mental processes that we experience with the somewhat consistent, enfleshed, and historically bound biological system that we call our body. Perhaps the most rigid form of Learning II is the illusion that a single system or mind abides in this entity that we call the body. We, as human beings, are in an awkward position. For reasons of physical efficiency and even survival, we are simultaneously compelled to operate under this illusion and to be challenged by our ongoing experiences to see its insubstantiality. Put in theological terms from our tradition, we are both physical and spiritual beings. To stay too attached to either aspect of being may cause more pain and suffering for ourselves and others. Learning III and IV provide us with processes to free our attention—not to be captured by any single mental process. I agree with Jacob Needleman that those in our tradition are called to an "intermediate Christianity,"[34] a between-ness that bridges between the one we call our self and the multiple others who are also sharing our common mental processes.

I believe that Bateson's notion of mind and of learning provides us with one language to examine just such between-nesses. The "*trans*" in transpersonal then becomes the placeless place where we are called to reflect on transformation. This placeless place is characterized by Learning IV. The "*trans*" in transpersonal is also the placeless place where we are called to action. I agree with Berman's concerns that mental process, in itself and narrowly construed, can become one more disembodied single vision.[35] It is precisely the processes of engaged living and intentional reflection in many religious traditions that can be informed by Bateson's ideas of mental process. Liberation theologians call this process "praxis" and stress the importance of specific concrete action—often in situations of great uncertainty and of danger (powerful between-ness, indeed)—with intentional community reflection.

Learning to be in this between-ness, to understand that our actions and our reflections are in resonance with all of God's creation, is not simply acting or not acting as individuals. For Christians following the spiritual journey, our faith-walk is in this between-ness. Our deepening relationship with God is a continuing lure to remain with God in this between-ness of relationship and to go deeply with the mystery that is God.

As Douglas Flemons concluded in his recent book looking at the relationship between Bateson's work and a different religious tradition, the Tao:

> The real work, the disciplined play of not-acting, connects separations and separates connections with the indifferent commitment of an imaginative rigor and the committed indifference of a rigorous imagination. Mind—living—resides in the relation between.[36]

It seems to me that one valuable way that we can define transpersonal psychology is as the praxis of such between-ness.

An earlier version of this chapter, "Gregory Bateson's Notions of Mind: Implications for Transpersonal Psychology: One Basis for Interfaith Dialogue," was presented at the 1993 Parliament of the World's Religions Academy, September 3, 1993, in Chicago, Illinois.

1. See Thomas Keating, *Open Mind, Open Heart: The Contemplative Dimension of the Gospel* (New York: Continuum, 1993).
2. George F. Cairns, "Introducing Centering Prayer into the Curriculum of an Ecumenical Seminary: A Call to Personal and Systemic Conversion," in *The*

Diversity of Centering Prayer, Gustave Reininger, ed. (New York: Continuum, 1999), 111–22.

3.   Ken Wilber is an extremely prolific writer. See a recent comprehensive overview of his thought in *Sex, Ecology, Spirituality: The Spirit of Evolution* (Boston: Shambhala, 1995).

4.   *The Journal of Transpersonal Psychology* is a central resource documenting contributions in this emerging field.

5.   Anthony J. Sutich, "Some Considerations Regarding Transpersonal Psychology," *Journal of Transpersonal Psychology* 1:1 (Spring 1969), 16.

6.   Ibid.

7.   Denise H. Lajoie and S. I. Shapiro, "Definitions of Transpersonal Psychology: The First Twenty-Three Years," *The Journal of Transpersonal Psychology* 24:1 (Summer 1992), 90–91.

8.   Here are Gregory Bateson's criteria for mind from *Mind and Nature: A Necessary Unity* (New York: Dutton, 1979), 92:

   1. A mind is an aggregate of interacting parts or components.

   2. The interaction between parts of mind is triggered by difference, and difference is a nonsubstantial phenomenon not located in space or time; difference is related to negentropy and entropy rather than to energy.

   3. Mental process requires collateral energy.

   4. Mental process requires circular (or more complex) chains of determination.

   5. In mental processes, the effects of difference are to be regarded as transforms (i.e., coded versions) of events which preceded them. The rules of such transformation must be comparatively stable (i.e., more stable than the content) but are themselves subject to transformation.

   6. The description and classification of these processes of transformation disclose a hierarchy of logical types immanent in the phenomena.

9.   Gregory Bateson and Mary Catherine Bateson, *Angels Fear: Towards an Epistemology of the Sacred* (New York: Macmillan, 1987), 19.

10. George F. Cairns, "Some Thoughts on Interpenetration: A Response to Angels Fear," *Continuing the Conversation* 10 (Fall 1987), 6–7.

11. Thomas Keating, "The Method of Centering Prayer," an undated brochure available from Contemplative Outreach Limited in Butler, New Jersey, or visit their website at www.contemplativeoutreach.org.

12. There are many expressions of this experience. See Richard Woods, *Mysterion: An Approach to Mystical Spirituality* (Chicago: Thomas More Press, 1981), for one helpful examination of the range of these experiences.

13. Fritjof Capra, David Steindl-Rast, and Thomas Matus, *Belonging to the Universe: Explorations on the Frontiers of Science and Spirituality* (San Francisco: HarperSanFrancisco, 1991).

14. For a detailed discussion of the contemplative dimensions of Christian community centered in liturgy, see Thomas Keating, *The Mystery of Christ: The Liturgy as Christian Experience* (New York: Continuum, 1993).

15. I described the experiences of one such community in "Establishing Base Communities in Uptown Chicago: Preliminary Reflections on a Ministry," *The Chicago Theological Seminary Register* 81:1 (Winter 1991), 34–41.

16. I am indebted to the work of Morris Berman, which encouraged me to examine Gregory Bateson's ideas regarding education and learning. In particular, his distillation of Bateson's work in *The Reenchantment of the World* (Ithaca, NY: Cornell University Press, 1981), provided me with the basis for many of the insights that follow in this section. An earlier version of this discussion of the theory of logical types appeared in my "Thoughts on a Praxis of Transformative Education," in *Theology and the Human Spirit: Essays in Honor of Perry D. LeFevre*, Susan Brooks Thistlethwaite and Theodore W. Jennings, eds. (Chicago: Exploration Press, 1994).

17. Gregory Bateson, *Steps to an Ecology of Mind: Collected Essays in Anthropology, Psychiatry, Evolution, and Epistemology* (Northvale, NJ, and London: Jason Aronson, 1972, 1987), 279.

18. Ibid., 280.

19. Here language poses difficulties. "Higher" and "lower" carry much surplus meaning, with "higher" suggesting "better" or more "spiritual" values and "lower" suggesting "poorer" or more "profane" ones. Not understanding that all levels of learning are always available to us has caused countless suffering and misplaced effort. Just as the class "furniture" is no better or worse than the subclass included within it, "table," so too Learning III and IV are no better or worse than Learning I or II. All are part of the human experience and equally important. It is *precisely the awareness that this is the case* that is difficult for us profoundly to experience and understand.

20. Bateson, *Steps to an Ecology of Mind*, 287.

21. Ibid., 292–93.

22. Ibid., 300.

23. Ibid.

24. Ibid., 301.

25. Ibid., 297.

26. Thomas Keating, *Invitation to Love: The Way of Christian Contemplation* (New York: Continuum, 1993), 5–18.

27. Ibid., 19–25.
28. Ibid., 145.
29. Bateson, *Steps to an Ecology of Mind*, 293.
30. Ibid., 301.
31. Gerald G. May, *Will and Spirit: A Contemplative Psychology* (New York: HarperCollins, 1982, 1987), 64.
32. Cairns, "Thoughts on a Praxis of Transformative Education," *passim*.
33. Keating, *Invitation to Love*, 147.
34. Jacob Needleman, *Lost Christianity: A Journey of Rediscovery* (Garden City, NY: Doubleday, 1980).
35. Morris Berman, "The Cybernetic Dream of the Twenty-First Century," *Journal of Humanistic Psychology* 26:2 (Spring 1986), 24–51.
36. Douglas G. Flemons, *Completing Distinctions: Interweaving the Ideas of Gregory Bateson and Taoism into a Unique Approach to Therapy* (Boston: Shambhala, 1991), 137.

Gail Fitzpatrick-Hopler

The Spiritual Network of
Contemplative Outreach Limited

THIS HISTORY AND EVOLUTION OF THE CONTEM-
plative Outreach organization demonstrate to me the remark-
able ways in which God orchestrates our lives, if we let go. My
life has been transformed through my experience and
commitment to live a contemplative life in the marketplace
with the support of this wonderful community without walls.
I have seen Contemplative Outreach grow and expand from
1983 to the present in amazing ways. Many people have
shaped this network—some of them have been with us from
the beginning, others have recently joined us, and still others
have made their contributions and moved on. Each has been
essential to the ongoing process of growth and transforma-

tion. The image of a group sculpting clay lends itself to the organic way in which Contemplative Outreach was formed. Often, while one area was being defined and refined, another was being shaped. Father Thomas Keating has been the spiritual animator and wisdom figure of this project from the beginning. His guidance and formation, along with his published works and videotape series, provide the main content for our workshops, retreats, and ongoing programs. Our experience has not followed a recipe or a prescribed set of how-tos; rather, we have tried to listen, to wait upon the movements of the Holy Spirit, and to consent.

An image that comes to mind when I think of the many faces of Contemplative Outreach is that of a mosaic picturing the Savior, a mosaic made up of hundreds of pieces of stone. Some stones are ordinary and others precious. Some are smooth and others rough. They are various colors—bright blue, red, yellow, dull green, warm purple, shiny black, and gold. As individual stones we can do little with them. Together, however, each is indispensable and makes a unique contribution to portray the face of Christ.

Members of Contemplative Outreach come from every walk of life. We are women and men interested in living a contemplative life in contemporary society. We touch people of all faiths and all denominations, and we recognize that there is unity in prayer. We are united in our goal to renew the contemplative dimension of the Gospel in daily life through the practice of Centering Prayer and *lectio divina*. In the words of our vision statement,

> Contemplative Outreach is a spiritual network of individuals and small faith communities committed to living the contemplative dimension of the Gospel in everyday life through the practice of Centering Prayer. The contemplative dimension of the Gospel manifests itself in an ever-deepening union with the living Christ and the practical caring for others that flows from that relationship.
>
> Our purpose is to share the method of Centering Prayer and its immediate conceptual background. We also encourage the practice of *Lectio Divina*, particularly its movement into contemplative prayer, which a regular and established practice of Centering Prayer facilitates.
>
> We identify with the Christian contemplative heritage. While we are formed by our respective denominations, we are united in our common search for God and the experience of the living Christ through Centering Prayer. We affirm our solidarity with the contemplative dimension of other religions and sacred traditions, with the needs and rights of the whole human family, and with all creation.

How did this movement of the Holy Spirit come about? Why did it happen at this particular time? Two important events happened in the second half of the twentieth century, each seeming to move monastic life out of the cloister and into the world: Vatican II in the West, and the exile of the Dalai Lama in the East. The doors of interreligious dialogue opened for the first time, and the contemplative values of silence, simplicity, and solitude were shared with ordinary people who were seeking a deeper relationship with themselves, with other persons, and, most importantly, with God.

Like a weaving, Contemplative Outreach came together with different textures, threads, fabric, and yarn in various colors. Three, however, are basic.

The first thread was a hidden treasure buried at St. Joseph's Abbey in Spencer, Massachusetts, in the early 1970s, where Fathers Basil Pennington, William Meninger, and Abbot Thomas Keating lived as contemplative monks. Vatican II opened doors for them that initiated a dialogue with other contemplative monks from the East and West. Through the dialogue, they became interested in sharing the monastic treasures of contemplative prayer with individuals seeking silence and the fruit of silence. The monks did not have much experience in teaching contemplative prayer. Their way of life was total immersion in prayer—in the words of Saint Benedict, "Prayer without ceasing." It was not easy for them to translate this into a model for lay use outside the cloister.

Father William Meninger was guest master at St. Joseph's Abbey and had studied the fourteenth-century classic, *The Cloud of Unknowing*, describing a lifestyle for deepening one's relationship with God through contemplation. He extracted from *The Cloud* a method of silent prayer that could be taught in a couple of hours. The method, called "The Prayer of *The Cloud*," had four simple guidelines. Meninger began to experiment at first by teaching priests who came to the monastery for retreats. It was understood that this prayer could not be learned from reading or studying; rather, it needed to be practiced in a methodical way. Meninger encouraged the retreatants to practice at least twice a day for twenty minutes each time. This was not to take the place of other kinds of prayer; it simply offered a method by which to practice silent prayer, a way of listening to God beyond words, thoughts, images, or perceptions. As more people heard of this method, they wanted to try it.

At the same time, Father Basil Pennington was being invited to give retreats to priests and sisters in their home monasteries and convents, and he also taught "The Prayer of *The Cloud*." While Pennington was giving a retreat at the Conference of Major Superiors of Men and Women, someone suggested to him that the name of the prayer should be changed from "The Prayer of *The Cloud*" to "Centering Prayer" because it put into a simple method something to which Thomas Merton had made allusions in his writings. It was a method to facilitate going into the center of one's being in order to be present to the presence of God within. From then on "The Prayer of *The Cloud*" was known as Centering Prayer.

Thomas Keating, as Spencer's abbot, encouraged the work. In 1977, he helped to develop a workshop for training teachers of Centering Prayer. Several people were trained at St. Joseph's Abbey and began to teach Centering Prayer to others. When Keating retired as abbot in September 1981, the retreats were discontinued. The people who had been trained at St. Joseph's kept on teaching Centering Prayer. Keating moved to St. Benedict's monastery in Snowmass, Colorado, to enjoy retirement as a monk. Shortly after his arrival in Snowmass, he was invited to give a Centering Prayer workshop in the neighboring town of Basalt—eighty people showed up on a cold winter night to learn Centering Prayer. This was a confirmation for Keating that the Spirit had something in mind.

The second thread started back in August 1983, when Keating gave the first "intensive" Centering Prayer retreat at the Lama Foundation in San Cristobal, New Mexico. This retreat emphasized extended periods of Centering Prayer. Keating also offered two presentations each day on the conceptual background in the Christian contemplative tradition, in concert with contemporary psychology and the spiritual disciplines of other world religions. I was one of twelve who were invited to attend this retreat. Among other retreatants at the Lama Foundation retreat who continued to work with us were Father Carl Arico, Father William Sheehan, David Frenette, Carl Shelton, and Mary Mrozowski (who died in 1993). Patricia Johnson and Mary Anne Matheson, both members of the Lama Foundation community at that time, served the retreat and are currently serving retreats at St. Benedict's Monastery.

This retreat was a heart-opening experience, and several of us made personal commitments to a daily practice of Centering Prayer; others began to teach Centering Prayer. The Lama Foundation offered another intensive Centering Prayer retreat the following year. Among its participants was Gustave Reininger, who had met Keating and his friend Edward Bednar previously in New York, where they had talked about the possibility of a contemplative network. While back in New York, Bednar wrote a grant proposal and received funds to start up parish-based programs in New York City that offered introductions to Centering Prayer. Bednar called his proposal "Contemplative Outreach," and thus the name was born. Bednar's image of this network was of a group of seekers united in their common search for a deep relationship with God through Centering Prayer in dialogue with world religions. Keating, Reininger, and Bednar organized several in-city Centering Prayer retreats. This activity marked the beginning of the Contemplative Outreach Centering Prayer Program. At the same time Bednar was serving Contemplative Outreach as its first executive director. Early in 1985, Bednar left this position, and Mary Mrozowski succeeded him.

Meanwhile, efforts were made in Colorado to establish a live-in community. The experiment disbanded early in 1985, but two of the members, David Frenette and Bob Bartel, moved east, joined Mary Mrozowski, and began again. During those early years the live-in community took a prominent role in the growth of Contemplative Outreach because it provided a consistent and established place to hold ongoing workshops and retreats of various lengths. Mrozowski, Frenette, and Bartel staffed weekend retreats, weekend introductions to Centering Prayer, and ten-day intensive retreats. The community at first lived in West Cornwall, Connecticut, and eventually settled in Warwick, New York, where it existed for ten years as Chrysalis House. Cathy McCarthy joined the community in 1988. Chrysalis House closed in 1996, but McCarthy carries on the work of Contemplative Outreach at St. Andrew's Retreat House in Walden, New York, where she hosts people from our worldwide Contemplative Outreach network.

In order to give herself to full-time community work, Mrozowski resigned the position of executive director in July 1986, and I have held that position since then. My coworkers and I shared an office space and held our board meetings at the Merton Center in New York City from 1985 to 1986. The board supported Keating's work and helped to develop materials and a basic delivery system for the introductory workshops. We offered Centering Prayer workshops when invited to do so. Once, we were invited to give a seven-week course at St. Francis Assisi Church on 31st Street in New York City. Our format was simple: a twenty-minute lecture on one of the aspects of Centering Prayer, a twenty-minute period of Centering Prayer, and group sharing. Invitations to present more workshops were extended to us by word of mouth. Our little board of directors was the nucleus of the movement, which meant we did all the work. We did not promote what we were doing, but we were constantly busy giving free workshops. *Open Mind, Open Heart* by Thomas Keating was published early in 1986 by Amity House and then republished by Continuum Press in 1993, and we used this book as our main resource, from which we developed lecture outlines and the basic essentials for the introductory workshops, follow-up sessions, and ongoing Centering Prayer groups. We still use the outlines today, although in a somewhat refined version.

The third thread of our weaving began in April 1986, when Contemplative Outreach became a New York corporation and the name "Contemplative Outreach Limited" was born. This corporation was founded to serve as an information and resource center for the spiritual network of Contemplative Outreach. At the end of 1986, we moved to the

Shalom Center in Englewood Cliffs, New Jersey, the Mother House of the Sisters of St. Joseph of Peace. In 1987, however, we moved again because the sisters needed space to expand their programs. I took my file box, telephone answering machine, and portable typewriter, and I set up the office on a dining room table in my home in Butler, New Jersey. In February 1988, the office outgrew its table, and we moved into my one-hundred-year-old one-car garage (277 sq. ft.). In 1997, we moved into a professional space in a renovated mill building in the downtown area of Butler. We now have 1250 square feet of space: five good-sized rooms and eight workstations. We have three full-time employees and one part-time employee. Today our office is the international headquarters for the network.

Although we held regular meetings since 1984, the first official board of directors was named in 1986 when the organization was incorporated. Our board included Thomas Keating, president; Carl Arico, vice-president; and Gustave Reininger, treasurer. Mary Mrozowski and I served as directors. This network has been a grassroots movement from the beginning and continues to grow from the bottom up.

Patricia Johnson and Mary Ann Matheson have staffed our intensive retreats at St. Benedict's Monastery in Snowmass, Colorado, since 1987. At first the retreats were offered annually but now are offered monthly. These retreats draw seekers from all over the world.

Interest in Centering Prayer appeared in many areas of the United States. For example, Father William Sheehan taught Centering Prayer in the Florida area from 1983 onward. He worked with volunteers interested in supporting the Centering Prayer movement and offered workshops and retreats. Many Centering Prayer groups were established in Florida, and they became one of the first Contemplative Outreach chapters. Similarly, other chapters appeared from grassroot movements, generally through the inspiration of one individual with an open heart and a willingness to share the experience with others.

In 1987, Francis Stafford, the Roman Catholic archbishop of Denver, Colorado, invited Keating to offer parish programs on Centering Prayer as a follow-up to their renewal program to all the parishes in the Denver archdiocese. Sister Bernadette Teasdale was hired by the archdiocese to coordinate the programs. This was the first diocesan-wide systematic and intentional approach to teaching Centering Prayer. For a period of time, the Center for Contemplative Living shared space with Christ-Centered Ministries, an Episcopal contemplative community founded by Canon David Morgan. Today, Sister Bernadette serves as a coordinator and faculty member for Contemplative Outreach. She directs the Center for Contemplative Living in Denver where many of the Contemplative Outreach programs, workshops, and retreats are offered. Sister Bernadette has a volunteer staff of fifty-one workers committed to Centering Prayer who run the center.

The center is self-sustaining and is located in a renovated convent in Denver.

It became apparent that we had to train individuals to offer the introductory workshop to Centering Prayer, and Keating appointed a faculty made up of people who had been teaching Centering Prayer since the early years. Over the years the faculty trained and commissioned some 700 individuals to give introductory workshops and follow-up sessions on Centering Prayer. Many programs have been designed and developed, such as the "Post-Intensive Retreat," "Formation for Contemplative Service," "Advanced Retreat," "External Study Program," "The Living Flame" (a seven-month course), and "Contemplative Living" (a nine-month course). We also offer practices that bring the fruit of Centering Prayer into daily life: "The Welcoming Prayer Practice," "The Forgiveness Prayer," and "The Practice of Contemplative Service: Attention and Intention." Our most recent developments have been the design of introductory workshops and retreats that feature *lectio divina.*

Interest in the method of Centering Prayer has spread beyond the boundaries of the United States to the Dominican Republic, the Philippines, England, Ireland, and other European countries, as well as several Caribbean islands, Canada, Mexico, some Latin American countries, Asia, Australia, and South Africa. Specialized ministries have bloomed: the Hispanic extension *Contemplativa Interna-*

cionale, a flourishing prison ministry, and a course in the contemplative dimensions of the Twelve-Step program that is just beginning. In 1996, Contemplative Outreach received a grant from Trinity Episcopal Church in New York to offer nationwide programs for the Episcopal Church. Our programs were well-received and continue to grow within the Anglican communion. We have also ventured into cyberspace, creating a "homepage" on the Internet at www.contemplative-outreach.org. Our newsletter has reached a circulation of 40,000 copies. We have fifty-five active chapters throughout the world. The weaving together of the Contemplative Outreach network is an ever-growing work in progress in the artistic hands of the Spirit of God.

In my role as executive director, I have had the pleasure of working closely with Father Thomas Keating. He has been my teacher, mentor, and dear friend. We have had the opportunity to pray and work together over this labor of love called Contemplative Outreach. Through Keating's example, I believe I have begun to learn how to let go and follow the inspiration of the Spirit—waiting, listening, and watching for our next movement. As we continue to grow and share our vision with people seeking the values of silence, solitude, and simplicity, I wonder what the new millennium will have in store for Contemplative Outreach. In any case, I trust we will continue to follow the guidance of the Holy Spirit and, day by day, move gently into the mystery of the cloud of unknowing.

Paul David Lawson

Leadership and Change Through Contemplation: A Parish Perspective

ONE OF THE MOST POPULAR STORIES IN THE early church was the story of Antony as told by Athanasius. This story gripped the imagination of the ancient world. Antony's life became so famous and familiar that by 400 CE, only a few decades after its publication, it was already seen as a classic and Antony as a hero from the past.[1] The story is filled with drama, struggle, ghosts, travel, desert wastelands, the devil and demons, triumph, healing, miracles, and the presence of Christ. Before all this excitement could take place and, in particular, before Antony could become *Saint* Antony, one thing was required, and that was that Antony be convertible: that there be within Antony the environment for

change, the capacity for growth, and the will to begin a spiritual journey.[2] This journey began with reflection on the
scriptures and a spiritual practice.

Many churches and congregations are on a similar journey seeking health, growth, or change on an institutional
level. They look for these things in new programs or new
leaders. Before new leadership or programming can take
place, however, a fresh environment is needed within the
congregation. That new environment can be created out of
the spiritual discipline of Centering Prayer.

At around half-past four every day the mail carrier knocks
on the parish office door bringing a foot of mail for the church
office. Of that twelve inches of mail, about six inches are
flyers, brochures, booklets, and seminar announcements. All
promise to make St. Cross's a better parish or its pastor a
better priest. This barrage does not end with the mail. In this
electronic age there are also e-mails and facsimiles, each
promising the same thing—to make our parish and its ministers better, faster, stronger, happier, and healthier, provided
we buy that particular program for success.

Today's mail, for example, included "Fresh Ideas," "Trans-
ferable Truth," "Boomer-Oriented Worship," "Generation
Targeting," and "Same-Page Thinking." Will these programs
really do what they promise? Or will they be just another set
of programs for institutional happiness that do not work,
becoming instead programs for institutional failure? If priests

want to help their congregations to prosper, grow, and be healthy, what should they do? Which program should they buy? The answer is, not surprisingly, "none of the above."

Healthy and happy congregations depend not on programs and pastors but on emotional process and congregational relationships in Christ. This process and these relationships need to be strengthened, nurtured, and supported through a contemplative discipline. One such discipline is Centering Prayer. The Centering Prayer model of working with congregations involves both new ways of looking at them and old ways of working with what is seen in them.

A New View

Recent discoveries are leading us to new ways of perceiving the world. Some of these discoveries include the interconnection of all living things and nonlinear thinking. In the physical sciences, we learn of a quantum world in which relationships are the essence of reality. In the biological sciences, we learn of a world that is directly interconnected in all of its parts, from the cellular level to the human level, from cell systems to human-family systems.[3]

For the last couple of centuries, most social institutions and organizations, including churches, have drawn their *Weltanschauung*—their view of the world—from science. More precisely, the worldview currently espoused by most churches and church organizations comes from the Enlightenment. What this means for church organizations is that we try to manage by breaking things into parts rather than looking at the whole. A part can be a person, a group, a program, or even an object such as a building. We assume that parts are influenced by a direct exertion of force, either against an object or by one person against another.[4] We behave as if we live in a cause-and-effect universe. We continue to act in accordance with mechanistic assumptions as if the world were a clock.[5] Such a world would be filled with limits, boundaries, and direct causes. Modern science, however, posits a much different world.

How human beings apprehend and comprehend the physical world, and what we understand about the world that we apprehend, has changed radically throughout recorded history. Some scientists would have us believe that this change has been an orderly progression, a march of progress through recorded history: human beings at first understood only a few things; as more and more facts were assembled, that understanding gradually changed into a "true" understanding of reality. In fact, this has not been the case at all. Instead, the history of science tells us that humans have believed one thing and then, seemingly overnight, changed to an almost opposite view. Instead of gradual progression through a building up of facts following the scientific method, a reversal of belief happens through a flash of insight. A flat world becomes round; a world a few thousand years old becomes billions of years old; the Earth as the center of the universe becomes just another planet; particles become waves; and objects that appear solid contain more space than matter. What is true of the physical sciences is also true of the biological sciences. Humans, once viewed as distinct individuals different from other animals, become just another part of the food chain, products of evolution.[6]

There are implications for churches and congregations in these ways of viewing the world. Churches and congregations today are products of their past. The organizational structure is feudal, the church schools and their curricula are based on the industrial revolution's training methods for factory workers, and the buildings and worship services are products of nineteenth-century Europe. The Church could survive all of this if did not continue applying the same outdated viewpoints when attempting to change. Churches still attempt to effect change by fixing parts and replacing individuals. Ministers and congregations look for programs that will make their churches successful, but successful change and leadership will come only when the Church takes a more holistic approach and makes changes that are more in keeping with modern understandings of the world and how it works.

One more holistic approach would be to view the congregation as a whole, and then to try and work with that whole instead of the individual parts that make up a congregation. Instead of adding programs or seeking quick fixes, church leaders would work with the entire environment of the congregation. That would include congregations, ministers, programs, buildings, history, and all surrounding emotional and environmental forces.

Surprisingly, one of the great examples of this approach comes from the beginning of the twentieth century in the building of the Panama Canal.

The Panama Canal

The building of the Panama Canal was one of the greatest human feats of all times. The construction of the Panama Canal was not just an American adventure in engineering and building, but also a triumph of the human spirit and the ability to change an environment. This is the story.

The nineteenth century was an age of industry, science, and engineering. It was an age of progress where no problem was so great that it could not be solved by human industry. One of the problems to be solved was the connecting of the east and west coasts in the Americas, a way to join the two great oceans.

A Frenchman, Ferdinand de Lesseps, already had experience building the Suez Canal, and a French syndicate was formed to construct the canal in Central America. The shortest route but also the most difficult was through Panama. A plan was developed to build a sea-level canal through the isthmus. The most experienced people and the finest engineers of the day using the latest mechanical devices were assembled to build the canal. It would be a colossal failure. Over a period of ten years, more than 20,000 people died, fortunes were lost, and the government of France fell, but the canal was not built. "The Panama Problem," as it was called, was too great. Construction was stopped by swamps over eighty-feet deep, a river that could rise more than forty feet in twenty-four hours, ground too rocky to dig for any great distance, and a climate that produced smallpox, yellow fever, typhoid, and malaria. Canal diggers became grave diggers.

The United States of America would take over the construction of the canal at the beginning of the twentieth century and succeed because, not only would they build a canal, but they would change the environment of the country in which the canal was built. Ironically, it was a Frenchman, Baron Godin de Lepinay, who proposed changing the terrain of Panama, but unfortunately his advice went unheeded by his own countrymen.[7] The first task facing the American canal builders was to solve the disease problem even before construction began. To do that streets were paved, windows screened, water and sanitation projects completed, all standing water removed, marshes drained, brush cleared, and the Anopheles mosquito eradicated. Dr. William Gorgas had correctly envisioned that for the canal project to succeed the first priority was not construction but health and sanitation.

In order to build the canal itself, changes in the topography of Panama needed to be made. The Chagres River with its width of over three hundred feet and its propensity to rise rapidly seemed an insurmountable problem. The French effort had ended in one hundred and seventy-four inches of rain and a sea of mud. The ground itself was hard rock and difficult to dig. The solution was to change the land and turn Panama into Nicaragua by creating the largest man-made lake in the world. This would drastically reduce the amount of digging through rock that was needed and change the river flow from an impediment to the source of water for the dams that would create the lake. Ships could move at greater speed and pass one another on the lake rather than in a narrow canal.

The solution to the Panama problem in building an interoceanic canal was not found just with new technology, greater will power, better engineers, or more money, although some of these things were helpful. Rather, the solution rested with changing the environment in which the canal was to be built. If the environment had not been changed, all the new technology in the world would not have helped.

Similarly, successful ministry in the church does not begin with better programming, better ministers, more committed congregations, or politically correct positions, but rather with the environment in which the programs are instituted and in which the minister will work. With churches and congregations that are in trouble or not prospering, the question becomes how you change the environment of the church and congregation. The answer lies in how congregations function.

Understanding the Congregational Environment

In the case of the Panama Canal, John Stevens could not begin the great feats of engineering until William Gorgas had changed the environment in which the construction was to take place. Similarly, programs for church growth, ministry, study, and nurture cannot begin until the environment of the congregation is changed into one that supports those programs and the people who implement them.

Understanding how a congregation works involves new ways of thinking. One method that is particularly helpful is nonlinear thinking. Rather than considering the congregation as a machine that needs to be repaired or to have parts replaced, the congregation should be considered as a whole: the relationship among the parts of a whole is examined and the influence that the parts have on each other is considered. In linear thinking, A causes B; in nonlinear thinking, A and B influence each other.[8] To say A, B, and C cause D is still linear thinking because each is considered an independent actor, a lone agent, while, at the same time, they each contribute to cause D. Nonlinear thinking holds that A, B, C, and D all influence and have effects upon each other. Edwin Friedman wrote in his book *Generation to Generation*, "Each part of the system (including the effect itself, "E") is connected to, or can have its own effect upon, every other part."[9] To illustrate this understanding, Friedman used American football. Only a casual fan of the game believes that when the quarterback is sacked it is his fault alone, or when a pass is successfully completed the quarterback alone is responsible for the success of the play. In both cases, whether the play was a success or a failure, blockers had to block, decoys had to decoy, throwers had to throw, and catchers had to catch. In addition, coaches and assistants had to design plays and counterplays. For an individual play to be successful, that is, the pass caught or the quarterback sacked, it is necessary for hundreds of events to influence each other.

Nonlinear thinking emphasizes the whole rather than any individual part. It focuses on the parts only in their relationships to and within the whole. It is a way of thinking that concentrates on structure and environment rather than on symptoms, and on the way a part functions within a system rather than on the part itself. For a congregation to be successful (whether it is in starting a new ministry, embarking on a program of growth, or just putting on the Christmas fete or jumble sale) involves more than hard-working individuals or well-designed programs. Success is determined by the relationships among the parts of the whole and how they function together.

Some congregations seem to function well. In those congregations programs always seem to work, the pews are full, and there never seems to be a shortage of funds. In other congregations nothing seems to work. In these congregations ministers and parishioners come and go, the pews are sparsely occupied, programs do not work quite right, and every church meeting seems to become an opportunity to reenact a famous historical battle. When new programs are attempted, they are met with anxiety, reactivity, crisis, and sabotage.

In a congregational setting, causes for anxiety may be the retirement of a minister, the arrival of a new staff member, the death of a prominent lay leader, or just about any event that changes the relationships within the congregation. This anxiety can produce reactivity, that is, unthinking responses to perceived threats. That in turn can produce uproars over slights, bureaucratic entanglements, disruption, interference, retorts, and censorship of the opposition. Complete agreement becomes a supreme value in the congregation, and scapegoats are found for church problems. The leadership of the community becomes less imaginative and seeks to "go through the motions." Leaders themselves become indecisive and seek peace rather than progress. The least mature are selected for church positions, and the more mature members of the congregation do not even bother to run. Everyone in the parish seeks a quick fix.[10] Not all congregations fall into the extreme of becoming a toxic waste dump, but many hover on the edge of existence. Many never become dynamic power stations of ministry but instead focus most of their concern internally on survival. In this kind of environment, how can churches progress and move forward? How can the Gospel be preached and programs for ministry be created?

Changing the Congregational Environment

Programs for church growth, ministry, study, and nurture cannot begin until the environment of the congregation becomes one that supports those programs and the people who implement them. In *Generation to Generation*, Friedman proposes that congregations operate as a family system. That is, that the behavior of the individual cannot be understood apart from the family in which the individual exists.[11] Friedman goes on to say that everything that can be said about the emotional process in families may also be applied to congregations. This emotional process or field, according to Friedman, includes all thoughts, feelings, emotions, associations, and past connections. It also includes the genetic heritage of individuals and the emotional history of the group. Particularly significant are the conditions under which the group originally took shape and how the organization has dealt with transitions, changes, and loss during its history.[12] How an organization or congregation behaves toward its members, and its relationship with others outside the group, depends on this emotional process. Whether a congregation is open or

closed, accepts change or is rigid, grows or declines—all are
dependent on its emotional process. The emotional field is
the environment of the congregation. In this context, will
alone is no more helpful with congregations than it is with
individuals. The only effective agent of change is the grace of
God.

Thomas Keating in *Invitation to Love* describes something
that is similar to the emotional system when he writes about
emotional programs for happiness, afflictive emotions, and
the false-self system.[13] Emotional programs for happiness
derive from instinctual needs for power, control, affection,
esteem, and security that develop into centers of motivation
to which our feelings, thoughts, and behaviors gravitate.[14] The
afflictive emotions are the emotions of anger, grief, fear, pride,
greed, and envy that arise in us when our drives for happiness
are frustrated. The false-self system is an understanding of self
that is based on a human image rather than on the image of
God. The false self seeks to build its image by satisfying the
programs for happiness, which are needs for power, control,
affection, esteem, and security.

Keating describes the origins of this false-self system with
all of its afflictive emotions and programs for happiness in
three ways. Theologically, he says, it is the result of coming to
full reflective self-consciousness without the conviction or
experience of God. This is the human condition not knowing
where to find happiness and believing that it lies in these

programs for self-fulfillment and the attainment of material goods rather than in relationship with God. In social terms, Keating describes the false-self system in terms based on the work of Jean Piaget and John Bradshaw. In this model the programs for happiness develop out of the unmet needs a person has from childhood. For example, a child denied security in its early years would in adulthood strive for security at all costs and in all things. The last model that Keating uses is an evolutionary one. The drives and desires for happiness come out of the reptilian brain and its primitive instincts rather than the more recent mental egoic consciousness that moves beyond self and self-centered drives into full personhood—a personhood that involves looking at one's own being in relation to others.

Self-centered drives will not bring us happiness or even success because, in the last analysis, they do not rest in the truth: that all happiness comes from God, all security comes from God, and all worth comes from God, and not from the plans and programs of our own devising. "The human heart," writes Keating, "is designed for unlimited happiness—for limitless truth and for limitless love—and nothing less can satisfy."[15] What is needed to address this problem of the false self and the human condition is repentance, that is, a reorientation, a change in the direction in which happiness is sought. This change may be experienced, Keating says, through the process of divine therapy known as Centering Prayer.

Centering prayer is a contemporary form of prayer of the heart, a discipline designed to reduce obstacles to contemplative prayer. It brings the procedures found in the teachings of Christian spiritual masters of the past into the present. Centering prayer involves two twenty-minute periods of prayer each day. Of the prayer periods, Thomas R. Ward Jr. writes, "Twenty minutes are needed to establish the necessary level of interior silence and to get beyond superficial thoughts....Our attachment to thoughts draws us from the presence of God as we go about our lives in the world."[16] The actual method itself is described in Keating's book, *Open Heart, Open Mind*. It is a method, but it is also more than a method; it is itself a prayer. Centering prayer is designed to draw our attention away from our daily concerns and ordinary flow of thoughts into an awareness of the spiritual level of our being.[17]

Just as congregations have an emotional field as described by Friedman, congregations also develop the false-self systems—emotional programs for happiness and afflictive emotions—as described by Keating. All of these together form the environment of the congregation. Congregations, like individuals, develop a false-self system and programs for emotional happiness. In congregations that are toxic, depressed, lacking in self-esteem, or just unsuccessful, the congregational environment is, therefore, the place where healing begins.

The Spiritual Environment of the Congregation

Congregations, like individuals, develop a false-self system and programs for emotional happiness. This system is often developed out of the origins of the congregation itself. For example, a church that was created out of a power struggle where a group of members left one church to form their own congregation might be concerned generations later with issues relating to power. "St. Hilda's" was formed when dissident liberals from several congregations in a very conservative diocese formed their own church. Many years later the congregation still had problems with the diocese. Often, at diocesan convention, members from this church would loudly oppose any plan the bishop put forward even though the politics of the diocese and the congregation had long since changed.

A church that for many years led a marginal existence might, even after becoming large and wealthy, still have issues in the area of security. For example, "St. Bede's" was a church that was formed when some people in the community got together, took out second mortgages on their homes, and built a large church building, even though they had to use some lower quality materials because that was all they could afford. They built at just the right time, their church grew and prospered, and they became a very large church, but generations later they still worried about money. It did not matter that they had savings accounts, bonds, and stock portfolios. Vestry meeting after vestry meeting was taken up with financial matters. Proposals were made to cut the diocesan assessment and reduce clergy salaries.

A church that was formed in the shadows of a large congregation might have problems with esteem. "St. Bartholomew's" was a small Hispanic church a few blocks from the large Anglican church of "St. George's" in a small southwestern town. It had been formed years earlier when Hispanics were not welcomed at "St. George's." Even after one hundred years, "St. Bartholomew's" was little more than a mission. It rarely tried anything on its own, often sought diocesan help for programs that never quite got off the ground, and complained that "St. George's" never did anything for them because they were too busy starting missions in Africa. Clergy never stayed long, and an air of defeat hung over the church.

Desire for control, power, affection, and esteem can also be traced to the origins of congregations that were formed out of doctrinal or political differences. This false-self system often manifests itself in a congregation's description and identity. A church might describe itself as being the largest, most liberal church west of the Mississippi. Another might describe itself as being the most conservative or wealthiest congregation in the diocese. In Episcopal churches this is most often seen in the certainty of any given congregation that the way they do liturgy is the only correct way. A newcomer to one of these congregations would need to reform their own heretical liturgical practices. In some congregations people are willing to die over the placement of a candlestick or the wording in a stained glass window. All of these behaviors are part of the congregational false-self system—a mistaken view that the worth of a congregation lies in its size or the success of its programming.

Another way that the false-self system manifests itself in the congregation is in overidentification with cultural conditioning and group loyalties. Rather than take personal responsibility for a congregation's decisions and actions, congregations project their difficulties onto others and accept values from authority figures or peer organizations without examination. This results in the practices of blaming and scapegoating. Our church would be full if it were not for the liberal national church staff. Our church would be full if our energy had not been sapped by conservative malcontents. Our church would be full if there were not a bigger church up the block. Our church would be full if only it were not the only Episcopal church in town.

The practice of Centering Prayer within a congregation leads to the acceptance of responsibility for a church's decisions and actions among church members. In congregations that struggle or are torn by strife, changing the environment becomes the first step in a program of reclamation, healing, and rebirth. The healing of the false-self system and the replacement of a material identity can begin with a program of Centering Prayer.

The Effects of Centering Prayer on a Congregation

When individuals and groups in a congregation practice Centering Prayer, they open themselves to the presence of the risen Christ in their lives and in the life of their congregation. There is a process of interior transformation of attitudes and motivation into the mind of Christ.[18] The signs of the resurrection of Christ are experienced in the daily life of the congregation. The presence of Christ becomes more powerful and visible because of the contributions of interior silence brought by the Centering Prayer community into the congregational community as a whole. Thomas Keating writes, "Once we begin our spiritual journey, there is no longer merely private prayer. Our prayer becomes a participation in the groanings of the Spirit for all the intentions and needs of the human family."[19] During the prayer itself there is a sense of oneness with the congregational community and all of God's creation. Keating describes this as a feeling of bonding that is the heart and soul of a Christian community.[20]

In practical terms the congregation begins to reorient itself, outside of itself, to the concerns of others and to the

well-being of all the members of its community. The congregation no longer needs to look outside itself for worth or
value. The actual number of people practicing Centering
Prayer does not appear to make a difference in the beneficial
effects upon the congregation and its influence among its
members. This may be because Centering Prayer groups act as
leaven within the congregational structure. Numbers are not
as important as practice.

A Congregational Study

As an example, let us look at a particular congregation's experience. Grace Church just outside Chicago had not done well
over the last few decades.[21] There had been allegations of clergy misconduct and a church civil war. Over half of the
members of the congregation had moved to other churches in
the area. Those who remained broke into small special-inter-
est clusters and had little contact with each other. Their last
priest had stayed a little over a year before moving elsewhere.

Father Joe Knight had been a rural minister from a near-
by farming community and had taken the job at Grace
Church without knowing a great deal about it other than that
it was a mid-size parish in a good area. Father Knight had
been looking to move closer to an urban area as his five children got closer to school age, and Grace Church seemed to be
in a good neighborhood with great schools. When he arrived,
he found that the members of the congregation were not

speaking to each other—and they were not speaking to him either. One church member said to him, "There's no point in our getting too involved since you will probably be gone soon anyway."

Clearly, Knight thought, what was needed was some good programming. In his first year he started a new Bible study group, reorganized the youth group, brought back the Christ-mas pageant, held three retreats, and had focus groups with the neighborhood to find out what people wanted. None of these programs worked. The priest became anxious and the following year redoubled his efforts. His work week was now at seventy hours. His five children began putting a question mark after the word "Daddy" when they greeted him. The programs in the second year were no more successful than they had been in the first year. His stewardship campaign actually lost money. At the end of the second year, he attend-ed a workshop on Centering Prayer as part of a continuing education program and decided to begin the practice himself and start a group in his church.

The results were impressive. At the end of a year his own anxiety had lessened, and this led to a reduction in the over-all anxiety of the institution. Knight was not so much concerned with the success or failure of the programs as he was with the relationships among the people in those groups. He found his congregation more open to new ideas and to trying new things. More people volunteered for programs, and three members of his Centering Prayer group went on to become members of the vestry, one of them its senior warden. People had fun again at church. The small insular groups broke up as people went into new ministry. Some of the programs that failed earlier were now successful. What had changed? *The environment of the congregation had changed.*

Congregations, like the human beings that comprise them, can over the years develop a false-self system. Many times this system is developed at the time of origin of the church because of factors involved in the congregation's creation. Sometimes a false-self system can be developed because of events in the life of a church—seemingly trivial events may develop over time into institutional drives for happiness and success that, in fact, accomplish neither. New programming will not solve the problems created by this false-self system, but change can be accomplished through an intentional contemplative program such as Centering Prayer. The fruits of these prayers are not seen at the time of the praying, but rather over time throughout the life of the congregation—and in the lives of its membership.

1.   William A. Clebsch, in his preface to Athanasius's *The Life of Antony and the Letter to Marcellinus*, Robert C. Gregg, trans. (New York: Paulist, 1980), xiv.
2.   Ibid., xv.
3.   John Tyler Bonner, "Differentiation in Cellular Social and Family Systems," *Family Systems* 1:1 (Spring/Summer 1994), 20.

4. See, for example, Margaret J. Wheatley, *Leadership and the New Science: Learning About Organization from an Orderly Universe* (San Francisco: Berett-Koehler, 1992), 6.
5. Ibid., 26.
6. Polly D. Caskie, "What Kind of System is the Family?" *Family Systems* 1:1 (Spring/-Summer 1994), 14
7. David McCullough, *The Path Between the Seas: The Creation of the Panama Canal, 1870-1914* (New York: Simon and Schuster, 1977).
8. Peter Steinke, *How Your Church Family Works: Understanding Congregations as Emotional Systems* (Washington, DC: Alban Institute, 1993), 4.
9. Edwin H. Friedman, *Generation to Generation: Family Process in Church and Synagogue* (New York: Guilford, 1985), 15.
10. Edwin H. Friedman, *A Failure of Nerve: Leadership in the Age of the Quick Fix* (Bethesda, MD: The Edwin Friedman Estate, 1999), 115.
11. Friedman, *Generation to Generation*, 195.
12. Friedman, *A Failure of Nerve*, 171.
13. Thomas Keating, *Invitation to Love: The Way of Christian Contemplation* (New York: Continuum, 1993), 14.
14. Thomas Keating, *Intimacy with God* (New York: Crossroad, 1994), 163.
15. Keating, *Invitation to Love*, 8–9.
16. Thomas R. Ward Jr., "Centering Prayer: An Overview," *STR* 40:1 (Christmas 1996), 25.
17. Thomas Keating, *Open Heart, Open Mind: The Contemplative Dimension of the Gospel* (New York: Continuum, 1993).
18. Thomas Keating, *Intimacy with God*, 154.
19. Ibid.
20. Ibid.
21. The name and location of this congregation have been changed, but the situation and events were very real.

Thomas Keating

The Practice of Attention/Intention

THE PRACTICE OF CENTERING PRAYER, BUILT upon *lectio divina*, is based on a millennium of Christian contemplative tradition. The barriers that we have created and our own internal "noise," however, must be overcome before we can fully allow the silence of God to well up from within and heal us. Our spiritual journey, therefore, requires not only a practice like Centering Prayer leading to contemplation, but also practices for daily life such as methods of right attention (to what we are doing) and intention (to why we are doing it).

The teaching of the Divine Indwelling is a fundamental doctrine for the spiritual journey. The Father, the Son as the Eternal Word of the Father, and the Holy Spirit are present within us. These relationships, which are never separate in their unity, are forever interacting. The Father is the potentiality for all existence; the Son is the actuality of all possibilities of existence; and the Spirit is the love that motivates both. Love loving itself eternally in the Trinity is the basis of our own existence, the most intimate part of us, that which is most real in us, the part of us that is capable of infinite happiness through participation in the divine life.

The true self, that which we are trying to awaken through spiritual practice, is not separate from God. The true self is the divine manifesting itself in our uniqueness, in our talents, in our personal history, in our cultural conditioning, and in the rest of the complex factors that go into making up our conscious life and its manifestation in our various activities. In spite of the obstacles we place in opposition to that manifestation, the infinite tenderness of God is present in us right now. Because of what traditional theology calls the fallen human condition, however, we are out of touch with this enormous energy of love that is inviting us to participate.

This does not mean that we have no identity of our own. Nor does it mean total absorption into God, as it does in some Eastern traditions. It does not mean the total loss of self. We remain uniquely whoever we are in virtue of our creation, but there is no possessiveness toward that uniqueness. The movement of the Spirit prompts us to give back whatever we are, all that we are, as much as we are, and everything that we have received from God. To give all back to God in love is the work of everyday life.

Around the true self there is a circle of awareness that we might call our spiritual nature. It has two principal faculties, the passive intellect and the will-to-God. These are, respectively, the innate desire for infinite truth and the innate desire for boundless love. Because of our fallen human condition, we are not normally in touch with our spiritual nature. Unconnected, our actual psychological consciousness on a day-to-day level is a "home-made," false self manifesting itself and not God.

The spiritual journey begins when we become aware that our ordinary psychological consciousness is dominated by the false self with its programs for happiness and overidentification with our cultural conditioning. The spiritual journey involves an inner change of attitude beginning with the recognition of being out of contact with our spiritual nature and our true self, and taking means to return. Only then can our true self and the potentiality that God has given us to live the divine life be manifested. Contemplative service is action coming from the true self, from our inmost being.

To liberate our true self is an enormous undertaking, and it takes time. Centering prayer is completely at the service of this program of liberation. It would be a mistake to think of Centering Prayer as a mere rest period or a period of relaxation, although it sometimes provides these things. Neither is it a journey to bliss. You might find some bliss along the way, but you will also have to endure the wear and tear of the discipline of cultivating interior silence.

Thinking our usual thoughts is the chief way that human nature has devised for us to hide from the unconscious. When our minds begin to quiet down in Centering Prayer, up comes the emotional debris of a lifetime in the form of gradual (and sometimes dramatic) realizations of what the false self is. We also learn how this homemade self that we constructed in early childhood to deal with unbearable pain became misdirected into seeking substitutes for God. Images that do not really have any existence except in our imagination are projected on other people instead of facing head-on their source in ourselves.

Consider the Beatitudes (Matt. 5:3–12). The capacity to practice them are within us as part of our baptism. Similarly, the gifts and fruits of the Spirit enumerated by Paul in Galatians 5 are vibrating within us all the time. They are mediated through the various levels of the psyche so that we do not experience their power until they are awakened through the discipline of deep prayer. Of course, there are other ways that God has of awakening us to the divine. God is, for instance, perfectly free to reach up and pull us down into that area at any time, but we should not count on it. It is *better* to practice a discipline.

What would be an active discipline to assist our Centering Prayer, so that it does not become self-centered or a mere process of self-protection, so that it actually is the assimilation of the infinite tenderness of God living within us? In general, such a discipline might be called "contemplative service." I call it the "attention/intention practice."[1]

When we emerge from Centering Prayer, the present moment is what we confront when we open our eyes. We have been in the present moment of prayer when we were completely open to the divine life and action with us. Then we get out of our chair and continue daily life. This is where attentiveness to the content of the present moment is a way of putting order into the myriad occupations, thoughts, and events of daily life. Attention to this context simply means to do what we are doing. This was one of the principal recommendations of the Desert Fathers and Mothers of the fourth century. The disciple would come for instruction and say, "I am interested in finding the true self and becoming a contemplative. What should I do?" The desert guides would reply in the most prosaic language, "Do what you're doing," which means, bring your attention to the present moment and its immediate context and keep it there. For instance, it is time for supper. Well, put the food on the table. This is true virtue. Turning on the television at that time or making a needless phone call might not be. Attending to the present moment means that our mind is on what we are doing as we go through the day. We are thus united to God in the present moment instead of wondering about what we are going to do next or tomorrow. There might be an appropriate time to set aside for planning, but not now.

To be completely present to someone with whom you are talking is one of the most difficult of all practices. Your presence will often do more than what you say. It gives others a chance to be present to themselves. Moreover, if your presence is coming from a deep place within, the divine compassion that is inspiring you will be there for them in the degree that they are capable of receiving it.

To be totally present to children if you have them, to the elderly if you have them, to counselees if you have them, to the job of the present moment that needs a responsible fulfillment—this is what might be called how to act from the center, how to do contemplative service, how to put order into ordinary daily life by being present to the occupation of the present moment. This cuts off an enormous amount of needless reflection, projects of self-aggrandizement, and wondering what people are thinking of us.

If we refuse to think of anything except what we are doing or the person that we are with, we develop the habit of being present to the present moment. In a way, the present moment becomes as sacred as being in church. Far better to be present to your duty if you are a bartender than to be present in church and thinking about being in a bar. At least you are present to yourself when you are paying attention to what you are doing.

Attention, then, is a way of doing what we are doing. It cracks the crust of the false self (our psychological awareness of daily life) in which we are the center of the universe while everything else is circling around our particular needs or desires. The false self is an illusion, but unfortunately it is a heritage we all bring with us from early life.

A practice, then, of paying attention just to what we are doing for a certain part of the day for the love of God, disregarding every other thought, is a practical way of opening ourselves to a deeper level of contemplation. It will not work instantly, but regular practice has long-range effects. It might be called the *how* of activity.

The spiritual level is also healed of the false self by the why of what we are doing. Our intention to do what we are doing for the love of God powerfully connects us with the divine presence. The power of intention is immense. The will willing God actually enters into union with God although we may not consciously experience the effects of the union right away. My intention is why I am doing what I am doing.

Here is the practice: We choose a certain time to establish and renew our intention of doing some particular word for the love of God. Our minds are generally so scattered that we often forget. To have a set time or particularly activity when we do this deliberately as a daily practice will quickly demonstrate the influence of intentionality on the false self. Nobody does anything without a motive. We do not know why we are doing something unless we know both our conscious and unconscious motivation. For example, as soon as we start trying to do a particular job for the love of God, the motivation of the false self begins to arise: we may find ourselves acting out of jealousy, we may want to get even with someone who has wronged us, or we might try to get ahead in some situation and trample on someone else's rights. The galaxy of bad intentions motivated by the false self emerges even when we try to maintain a pure intention for a few minutes.

The great insight of the early Desert Fathers and Mothers was that a pure intention leads to purity of heart; selfish motivation is gradually eliminated and the habit of a pure intention is firmly established. We begin to enter into God's intentionality, which is to manifest infinite compassion in the present circumstances, however painful, however joyful, however seemingly bereft of the divine presence.

As soon as we focus our intention—*why* we are doing this particular action—our unconscious motivation arises. The unconscious motivation might be that in our service, however devoutly it may appear to others, what we are really seeking is praise. In other words, our secret desires begin to emerge into our consciousness when we deliberately focus our intention on loving God in all that we do.

How we work—attention. *Why* we work—intention. This leads to the third and final quality of contemplative service: *Who* is doing the work? Having uncovered the spiritual obstacles of pride, envy, and whatever else might be hidden in the unconscious, we are now approaching our true self. We are approaching our inmost center. We are approaching "Love loving itself." What is going to happen? Without *intending* anything special, without necessarily *doing* anything special, people begin to find God in us as we humbly do what we are supposed to be doing. Complete submission to God allows the divine energy to radiate, and others seeing this have a sense of being in touch with God or in the midst of a community where divine love exists. This is what a Christian community is supposed to be, whether it is a family, parish, or organization. This third way of working or acting in daily life might be called "transmission."

When attention to the present moment and a pure intention are established as habits, then we have, in the fullest sense of the word, contemplative service. Our contemplation is thus perceived, enjoyed, and received, perhaps without a word being spoken, or without anyone being able to explain it. People know that, somehow, Christ is active and present in us—and loving *them* through us. This is the atmosphere in which people can grow and become fully alive. One needs to feel loved as a human being to come alive. The greatest love, of course, is divine love, especially when it becomes transparent in others. And divine love is most impressive when such persons are not even aware of it, when that love just happens.

------

1. This practice was first developed at Chrysalis House, Warwick, NY, especially by David Frenette, one of its charter members.

About Contemplative Outreach Limited

ESTABLISHED IN 1984 AS A PARTNERSHIP BETWEEN laity and monastics, Contemplative Outreach is committed to renewing the contemplative dimension of the gospel for those in active life. Contemplative Outreach affirms the Christian contemplative tradition from which Centering Prayer is drawn, and recognizes this tradition as a common ground for Christian unity. Its primary focus is to present the method of Centering Prayer and to offer practices that bring its fruits into daily life. Also encouraged is the dynamic process of *lectio divina*—scripturally based prayer—particularly its transition into contemplative prayer.

Contemplative Outreach offers introductory workshops, intensive prayer retreats, and contemplative service formation. For more information, please call 973-838-3384 or fax

973-492-5795. Contemplative Outreach Ltd. may also be
contacted over the Internet at:

www.contemplativeoutreach.org.

Or write to:

Contemplative Outreach Ltd.

10 Park Place, Suite 2B

P.O. Box 737

Butler NJ 07405